One of the keys to succ
effectively market our
relationships with our customers. As the level of change an
competition intensifies in the dental profession, it is critical now
more than ever to focus on these key areas of business success.

*Fully Booked – Dental marketing secrets for a full appointment
book* provides a step-by-step guide covering the core fundamentals
of a successful dental practice marketing plan. It takes out the
complexity and jargon and provides a realistic, tangible and
implementable approach for any practice looking for success.

This book is a must read for any current or new practice owners,
principal, practice managers or those involved in running a dental
practice and wanting to take their practice and patient relationships
to the next level.

Michael Fahey, National Sales Director, Henry Schein Halas

In the ten years I've been the editor of *Bite* dental magazine, I've
come across quite a few marketing 'experts' – some legitimate,
many not. Carolyn S Dean is one of the former – the real deal when
it comes to marketing expertise, which you can tell by reading this
book.

The advice in *Fully Booked* is spot-on, is specifically tailored to
dental practices, and is wonderfully comprehensive. I love the
checklists at the end of each chapter, which help you keep up with
a lot of detailed, smart and actionable information.

For any dentist concerned with attracting and keeping patients in
this day and age, *Fully Booked* is a must-read.

Rob Johnson, Editor, *Bite* Dental Magazine

The reality is the practices that Software of Excellence work with have limited experience and expertise when it comes to running a dental practice as a business. As the world of running a dental practice gets more competitive and complicated it is critical to understand the key elements that are going to make you successful and move from a good practice into a great business.

This book gives a fantastic overview of marketing, breaking down the jargon and highlighting the key aspects that you need to understand and implement to grow your practice.This is a must read book and highly recommended to everyone involved in developing a successful dental practice.

Jonathan Engle, General Manager APAC/International Marketing Director, Software of Excellence

In *Fully Booked*, Carolyn S Dean has produced an invaluable read and reference for dental practice owners and practice managers. If you want to get serious about marketing in dentistry and especially the new expanding world of online presence, then start here! From basic concepts and expanding to a well-structured step-by-step plan, Carolyn guides the reader with experience and skill on the road to success.

I highly recommend her book, well done Carolyn!

Dr. Frank Papadopoulos, Dentist and Founding Co-Director Centaur Software – Dental4Windows SQL/MediaSuite

A refreshing idea that is long overdue!

When we study to become dental professionals, we learn all aspects of work within our scope. We become competent in daily practice but not, unfortunately, business generation and best practice. This book is unique in that it gives insights, common and revolutionary, to maximize our working day. It does this by putting forward ideas that can help market your practice, fill patient appointment books and maintain patient retention allowing us to do what it is we love to do, treat patients!

Fully Booked is recommended reading for all dental prosthetists, dentists, dental hygienists and therapists, practice managers and people interested in great ideas to maximise business outcomes.

Abe Awakian, President, ADPA NSW

I have floundered around with marketing for my dental practice over the years. The organisations I have used to help me, with hindsight, have not really had a clue about marketing a dental practice & the results I have achieved have been random and disappointing; invariably leaving me with the feeling that someone other than myself has profited from the exercise.

Using Carolyn S Dean's team to market my dental practice is a no brainer. I find I am several steps ahead with each marketing project because My Dental Marketing understands the dental industry from top to bottom and has a compelling solution, backed up with data and results from campaigns run in similar "dental" circumstances. Why spend your time and your money inventing a surf board when clever people like Carolyn Dean are already here riding the wave for you.

Dr. Andrea Clarke BDS, Milford Dentists and
Hobsonville Point Dental, Auckland

Carolyn S Dean has demystified the cloud of noise that is marketing. In *Fully Booked*, she sets up clear pathways to enhance your dental practice using the latest marketing techniques.

Fully Booked starts by showing you how to clarify the core reason that you are in practice along with your passion and your 'why'. It then explains how to identify the 'DNA of your brand' and how to create targeted marketing campaigns to grow your dental practice and get more patients.

Whether you starting your dental practice from scratch or addressing your current position *Fully Booked* needs to be read.

Ian Shapland, National Business Development Manager, Elite Fitout Solutions and President, Australian Dental Industry Association (Queensland Branch)

Carolyn's latest book, *Fully Booked*, brings clarity to the murky waters of dental marketing. Her new book is a game changer to dentists in Australia.

As dentists in private practice, we can undertake the most complex of dental procedures in small dark spaces but are literally in the dark when in comes to the business side of our practices!

The moment I started reading Carolyn's book she made the daunting concepts associated with dental marketing coherent and intelligible. Her step by step process and writing style makes *Fully Booked* a joy to read and empowers me to dive in and explore the world of dental marketing so my practice can thrive with me at the helm.

Dr. Sara Lonergan, Tooth Sparkler Family Dental Care

When a great idea or a new book comes along people often say "why hasn't someone thought of that before?". This book goes much further than just attracting patients to your practice but makes you think about why you are in business and the importance of incorporating marketing into your overall business plan.

Most of the book is equally relevant to non-dental businesses and on that point I have had my business's website (MW Partners , Specialist Dental Accountants and Tax Advisers) established and maintained by My Dental Marketing.

With the business of dentistry becoming more competitive than ever, I believe this book is a must read for every dentist who wants to be educated on the core principle of marketing as part of a strategy to run a successful practice.

Albert Gigl, Principal, MW Partners – Specialist Dental Accountants and Tax Advisers

Over the last 10 years the face of Dentistry in Australia has gone through major change. There has been a large influx of foreign dentists and more dental schools have been built graduating far more dentists than the profession requires. Corporates have been allowed to purchase dental practices and with huge amounts of money behind them and business experience, they can weigh out market private practices. Combined with this, patients are more savy with their spending habits and more selective in who they go to for dental treatment. The internet revolution and easing of advertising restrictions has totally changed the way we need to market our practices. Certainly gone are the days we can just open our doors, do good quality dentistry and patients will flock to us. Most general private practices today are certainly struggling to keep their appointment books full.

So this timely book is a well thought out, comprehensive insight into the state of dentistry in Australia today explaining the steps necessary to succeed in marketing, getting and retaining patients.

With decades of experience in marketing as well as working with dentists and dental practices Carolyn is uniquely positioned to share her vast knowledge in this field.

Dr. Jeff Brown, Principal Dentist, Greenwood Dental

Fully Booked is a book filled with extensive dental marketing advice that is critical for any practice operating in today's competitive environment.

The nine-step process given in the book makes an easy to follow guide for topics like building the right team & brand for your practice.

I would highly recommend this book to any dentist who wants to grow their practice

Robert Bowles, Dental Fit Out

Carolyn S Dean's book is a must read for any dentist who is planning to flourish over the coming years. Her expertise and insight are real eye-openers to what many dentists consider the "Black Art" of Marketing. The nine step plan in *Fully Booked* is a road map to success that every dentist can follow.

Carolyn's wealth of industry knowledge positions this book as the premier publication for all Australian dentists.

Steve Daley, Director Healthcare Financial Strategies

Fully Booked is a much needed book for the dental industry and Carolyn S Dean is the perfect person to have written it.

Carolyn's wealth of knowledge and experience in the marketing of dental practices, especially in the realms of online opportunities, means she has become a highly sought after expert for dental surgeries. She gives insightful and practical advice throughout and her lessons for navigating online promotion of businesses. Her knowledge is invaluable.

I recommend this book to every dental practice, from start-ups through to well established surgeries. I know Carolyn to be very driven and focused and admire the success she generates in her life, and in the businesses she works with.

Julie Parker, Julie Parker Dental Management

This is a book that helps every day Aussie dentists decipher and survive the ever changing online marketing arena.

It is easy to read and very informative.

I have known Carolyn for many years, she setup my website and couldn't be more thankful for the great job.

Dr. Saif Hayek, Founder Advanced Dental Services

The success of your dental practice is significantly influenced by your marketing ability, however these skills are rarely taught at university. Carolyn's dental marketing book will help you overcome this shortfall by providing you with an accelerated marketing education. Carolyn has a rare ability to translate marketing speak into plain English, and provides a roadmap that will allow you to develop your dental practice to the level you would like it to be.

David Hazlewood, Dental and Medical Financial Planner
for Western Pacific Financial Group, Author of Clinical Trials
– *How Successful Doctors Navigate The Constantly Changing
Medical System To Achieve Financial Well Being*

At last an easy to read, practical book on Dental Marketing. With a strong focus on attracting new patients and keeping the current one's loyal, *Fully Booked – Dental marketing secrets for a full appointment book* is a great resource for every dental practice. It is filled with business building strategies that can be implemented immediately and are relevant in the Australian marketplace.

As a marketing professional for 25 years, and more recently business manager for Plateau Dental Care, I found working with Carolyn and her team invaluable. Her structured approach to marketing makes sense and is cost-effective.

In this competitive climate a proactive marketing plan is essential to business success.

Toni Black, Business Manager, Plateau Dental Care

Fully
Booked

Dental marketing
secrets for a full
appointment book

CAROLYN S. DEAN

www.fullybookeddentist.com
www.mydentalmarketing.com.au

First published in Australia by Carolyn S. Dean in 2016

ISBN: 978-0-9942897-0-4

Cover design by Boxer & Co.
Text design and book production by Michael Hanrahan Publishing

To Gerry, Callum and Ciara
for their endless love, support and
belief in me.

Please note

The advice offered in the book is general marketing advice. Before following this advice you need to check that you are operating within all regulatory frameworks.

Please conduct research and obtain advice on the relevant Federal, state and territory legislation that applies to your practice.

Contents

Foreword

If you had asked dentists in the graduating classes of 1970, 1980, or 1990 what marketing they were doing for their practices, the answers would have been very short.

They might have placed an ad in the Yellow Pages. There might have been a sign hanging down from the awning in front of their strip-shopping practice. There could have been a brass plate if they were in a professional building.

But that would have been it...at the most.

Marketing was actually even frowned upon. It was not only seen as the last bastion for dentists who couldn't get patients any other way, but also deemed inappropriate by the dental authorities.

The world of dentistry has changed a lot in the past few decades.

Those years have coincided with:

- The creation and growth of the Internet.
- An increase in the number of dental schools.

- An overcrowded marketplace, with most members of the dental profession thinking that there are too many dentists in practice.

- A rise in corporate dentistry, creating a whole new market of competition – one that is more able to cut its costs, *especially* in marketing. Many of the corporate entities in the dentistry business are owned by insurance companies. These companies market directly to *their* members...who just happen to be *your* patients.

All of these factors have changed the world of dentistry as we knew it, especially when it comes to marketing.

The overcrowded marketplace and rise in corporate dentistry mean that new practices are fighting hard to attract patients. It is no longer a matter of just opening the doors and waiting for the patients to find us.

Luckily for new practices (and older practices willing to adapt to changing technologies), there has been a simultaneous shift to the Internet when it comes to management of many aspects of business, especially marketing. This has meant that, provided a dentist can find his way in the world of dental marketing (navigating website design, pay per click advertising, search engine optimisation, blogs, forums, and algorithms), it is possible to establish a successful practice – even in a crowded marketplace.

However, being knowledgeable in the ways of dental marketing is a full-time job in itself, with rules constantly changing and a unique skill set required. The challenge of staying on top of this has become more and more sophisticated and is increasingly the realm of dental marketing specialists.

In my thirty-five years as a dentist, and more recently as Chairman of Prime Practice P/L, I have worked with many clients whose practices have benefited greatly from working with marketing companies that understand their needs and goals. I have also seen what can happen when a practice doesn't pay enough attention to what is now a vital part of running a dental business.

As the marketplace becomes more saturated, dental practices need to be proactive about having marketing strategies that not only make them stand out from the crowd, but also increase their patient-base and retention rates. Knowing who your market is, what they are reading, and which social media sites they are visiting is central to any marketing campaign. If you're putting out the right message, but it isn't reaching your audience, then the effort and time spent in crafting that message is wasted. Conversely, if your audience is hearing the wrong message, that can have a detrimental effect on your business's success. Knowing how to market, and to whom, is an integral part of running a successful, profitable practice in today's dental industry.

I can thoroughly recommend *Fully Booked* by Carolyn S Dean to any dentists who want to get to grips with their dental marketing and understand the essential elements required to promote their practice in the most effective manner.

In my experience of working with Carolyn and recommending her and her team's services to Prime Practice clients, I have found her to be an ethical, knowledgeable, and excellent consultant who specialises in dental marketing.

The steps outlined in the chapters to come shine a light on topics such as marketing touch points, practice branding, internet marketing, blogging and all the different types of internal and external marketing needed for a dental practice operating in today's competitive environment.

Using this knowledge and following Carolyn's advice will enable you to raise your business above the bar, increase your patient-base and stay ahead of your competition.

Whether you wish to outsource your marketing activities or improve them within your practice, arm yourself with the expert guidance in 'Fully Booked' and follow the steps to dental marketing success.

Dr. Phillip Palmer

Dr. Phillip Palmer ran a successful dental practice in the Sydney CBD for 34 years.

He has been involved in teaching dental practice management since 1995 and he is Chairman of Prime Practice Australia P/L.

Through Prime Practice, he has helped thousands of dentists to reach their goals, increase their income, and enjoy their practices more. He has lectured around the world on practice management topics and has a deep understanding of all the different management, financial and professional issues that face dentists. He is regarded as Australia's leading expert in the business of dentistry.

Introduction

Escaping an out-dated paradigm

When I talk to dentists, many of them express a desire for more new patients. But when I ask questions about what they are doing to attract patients to their practice, I am surprised to find so many dentists still stuck in an out-dated paradigm.

Up until twenty to twenty-five years ago, you were effectively not allowed to market yourself as a dentist in Australia. You could only make an announcement when you opened your practice and that was all. Your signage even had to be of a certain size and font. Because of this, many still consider it unethical or just wrong to market or advertise their dental services.

But times have changed. As a dental professional, you are facing unfamiliar challenges running and marketing your practice. You are confronting increased competition (both locally and abroad), an oversupply of dentists, ever-rising practice operating costs, and more marketing-savvy patients. On top of this, your potential patients are becoming more discerning about where they go to get dental services, with many heading overseas.

To achieve practice success, it is essential to build long-term relationships with patients and prospects. Long-term patients are more likely to feel satisfied. It is they who welcome the opportunity to refer others to you and who will continue to use your services in the future.

It is now more critical than ever for you to make informed choices regarding how to market your practice in order to consistently attract new patients and retain current ones.

The myth of the marketing silver bullet

Marketing your dental practice to attract the right kind of patients, keep them active, and get them to refer you to their contacts is no easy task.

The companies trying to sell you the 'marketing silver bullet' that will 'solve all your marketing worries' are constantly calling. Well-meaning friends, colleagues, and patients are giving you advice on what they think you should do to market your practice. The range of marketing media is evolving, and the rapid changes in online marketing make it almost impossible to keep up.

You want to be able to focus your main energy on running your dental practice, while employing the right marketing tools and techniques to ensure its success.

I have written this book to help dental professionals better understand how to effectively market their practice and build long-term relationships with their patients. You no longer have to work it out by yourself, filtering through multiple sources of advice.

The purpose of *Fully Booked* is to take the hard work out of dental marketing. Its nine-step process will work for any dental professional (practice owner, practice manager, or marketing consultant) who wants to grow their practice.

Dental marketing is not just about ads, email campaigns, or having a social media presence. It is about building and maintaining relationships with your patients.

Common dental marketing mistakes

Over my years working with hundreds of dentists as a marketing consultant, I have observed the common challenges that prevent them being able to successfully market their practices:

- They have few or no marketing skills, as dental schools around Australia still deliver very little in the way of business or marketing training.
- They have no overall marketing plan or strategy.
- They have been burned badly in the past with their marketing activities.
- They don't accept that they can and should market their practice and their services.

And what are the biggest mistakes that dental professionals are making when marketing their practice?

- They have a scattergun and inconsistent approach to marketing.

- They do not track the return on investment (ROI) of the marketing that they have done/are doing.

- They do not know the average lifetime value of a patient, which makes it incredibly hard to set a marketing budget and to think about long-term strategies.

- Because of the overwhelming amount of information, advice, and options when it comes to marketing, they often procrastinate and do nothing.

- They try and do it all themselves, taking shortcuts and trying to save money, resulting in failure and frustration.

- They fail to get the right expert advice, causing a cycle of disappointment. This often leaves them feeling fearful of attempting anything else.

- Many think that there is a 'silver bullet' to solve their marketing issues. This leaves them open to unscrupulous sales people, and to disillusionment and frustration when their marketing efforts fail.

So how can you overcome the long list of mistakes, wasted money, and wasted time? The nine steps I've identified not only give you an understanding of what you could be doing to market your practice, but also enable you to plan, track, and execute your marketing campaigns in an effective manner.

The nine-step process

STEP 1. Get back to basics

The first step addresses the basics of identifying your 'why' and what your core values are. Understanding your patients and knowing your competition are key to success.

STEP 2. Start with a plan

It is incredibly important that you have a marketing plan for your practice. If you don't plan then you are very likely courting failure, because you don't know where you're heading and can't evaluate whether your marketing attempts have been successful.

STEP 3. Build the right foundation

This step focuses on having the right foundation on which to build your practice. Your team and your brand are your keystones. An understanding of patient touch points and the different types of marketing are your launch pad.

STEP 4. Attract the right patients

Now that you have the right foundation, you can then target your ideal patient. This step is where you understand the right marketing tools, channels, and techniques to attract the right kind of patients to your practice.

STEP 5. Nurture relationships with your existing patients

Attracting patients to your practice is only the beginning. You need to understand how to build on the relationships with your existing patients by using the correct marketing tools and techniques to turn them into long-term patients.

STEP 6. Maximise your patient referrals

Long-term patients will always refer people to you. Developing referral programs maximises the benefits of word of mouth. In this step, you learn what makes a great referral program and how you can deliver this in your practice.

STEP 7. Foster partnerships and raise your profile

Once you are building great relationships with your patients, it is time to look outside of your practice and see what other businesses you can create partnerships and programs with.

STEP 8. Learn to listen

To understand what you are doing, both right and wrong, in your relationships with your patients, you need to learn to really listen and respond to them. With the advent of social media and online review websites, it is now easier then ever before to listen to your patients and learn from what they are saying. In this step, you will learn the best techniques and tools to enable you to listen well.

STEP 9. Review, revise, retry

As with everything in your practice, it is imperative to review your marketing. This step guides you through reflecting on what is and isn't working, revising anything that needs changing, and then retrying.

How to use this book

Each chapter of this book is written as a self-contained topic with exercises, cases studies, and checkpoints. You can, therefore, dip into the book at any point, but I recommend that you work through the steps one at a time, building upon a solid foundation.

This approach will be the difference between success and failure for any new or experienced dental professionals wishing to grow their practice. If you are serious about marketing your practice in a controlled and monitored way, not falling victim to unscrupulous providers, and being freed from the frustration of unsuccessful marketing efforts, then read on. It is time to change your mindset.

Changing your mindset

I understand why many of the dentists out there are still of the mindset that marketing is wrong. But many excellent dentists have realised that, to grow their practices, marketing is essential. To stay and flourish in business, you need to embrace marketing and recognise it as critical to your practice success.

There are some significant mindset changes that I believe need to be taken into account before we progress.

Dentistry is a business

Even though you are delivering an important service to the community, your dental practice is most definitely a business and, as such, requires sound business practices. The business of dentistry requires that you understand everything from bookkeeping to basic tax law, from marketing strategies to good record keeping.

Very good dentists are not necessarily equally good business people. It is widely recognised that business skills aren't taught in dental school, meaning new dentists are unprepared to run a business. Therefore, dentists tend to learn the hard way, through making mistakes. Many realise after a couple of years that there are aspects of dentistry they don't understand, such as how patients come and go from a practice, how to market a practice effectively, and how to employ and retain staff.

Successful dental practitioners hire coaches and experts, attend business seminars, read up on marketing business practices, join networking groups, and seek help to hone their business skills.

Those who do best at running a dental practice are those who are able to embrace the business end of things. They find gratification, even fun, in setting business goals and achieving them.

You are competing

The combination of the huge increase in the dentist to population ratio and the rapid expansion of national corporate dental centres will impact almost every dental practice in the country. More than ever, it will force dentists to compete for work and look for ways to stand out from the crowd.

You may consider the other dentists in your area to be your friends, and you are right. They are your colleagues, your allies, and maybe even your confidantes, but they are also your competitors. There are a finite number of potential patients in the area, and you are all fighting for a bigger piece of the pie. You and your practice are now in a highly competitive environment.

You need to be marketing

Relying on your current patient base and word of mouth is no longer good enough. In today's world, marketing and advertising are not only accepted but expected. Don't miss out because you view marketing as tarnishing your professional image. You can run a respected, professional business and still promote your practice and services to the community.

Your patient is always right

In today's highly competitive arena, it is imperative that you start listening to and understanding your existing and potential patients. For your practice to survive and thrive, the patients have to come first. You need to adapt your business to account for patients' needs, wants, and fears.

Patient education, sales, and communication are key

If marketing has a bad reputation, then sales is even worse. But we are now in a consumer age. Your patient today is more discerning and does not necessarily blindly follow your recommendations. Most dental treatment is discretionary and costs are high.

The reality of being in practice is that every time you get an enquiry and you respond, you are actually selling to the patient, i.e. convincing them that your dental services are right for them, that you are best positioned to deliver the services, and that you will deliver the service in a manner that is right for them. All of your staff members are your sales people, and your receptionist is your front line sales force.

I am by no means suggesting that you adopt a hard line style sales talk. Once the patient believes the dentist has a sales agenda, trust is quickly broken. No doubt, you have all had patients who have come to you having left the dentist who tried to sell them expensive treatment.

I suggest that you look at your team's communication skills and work on how you can communicate effectively with your patients, so they accept the treatment right for them. Communicate with your patients so that you can guide them through the various options to prevent objections, without being viewed as a salesperson.

You must abandon the silver bullet

I am sorry to say that there is no silver bullet solution to your marketing woes. There is really no single thing that you can do to guarantee attracting more new patients; likewise, there is no single thing that you can do to guarantee the retention of your patients.

The only true way to achieve marketing success with your practice is to introduce and refine upon multiple touch points (marketing communication activities) with your patients.

Marketing is everything... everything is marketing

When I talk to dentists, I notice there is still a common belief that marketing is all about advertising and selling. The truth is that marketing is not only advertising; it is not only selling. These are just a small part of what marketing is.

> Marketing is everything a practice does to educate existing and prospective patients about its services, from an advertisement in the local newspaper, practice brochures, website and online presence to patient communication and satisfaction.
>
> The key to great marketing and communication is finding out who your ideal patients are, working out how to reach them, and letting them know about your services.

It was Regis McKenna who coined the saying, 'Marketing is everything and everything is marketing' (Harvard Business Review). It was his way of expressing the fact that marketing is not a function but an all-pervasive way of doing business.

If you wish to grow a sustainable practice, now is the time for you to embrace marketing at the core of your business.

My story

You might be wondering why you should listen to me. My job and 'my passion' is to devote time to researching the latest dental marketing trends and best practice. I do this because most dental professionals like yourself are focused on the demands of running your business and don't have the time or inclination for intensive research on how to best market your practice. There is nothing I enjoy better than working with dental practices to help them to get their marketing working effectively. It's my job and I love it.

How this came to be my purpose makes a strange and interesting story. I came to Australia from the UK at the age of twenty-eight. I was doing incredibly well in my career in the high-end IT industry. It was the middle of the tech boom and life was great. I was young, smart and very hungry for success.

I feel blessed to have been part of the tech boom. The training I received within the corporate environment was quite honestly staggering. The blue chip IT companies that I was working for at the time had no limit to the amount of money they spent training and supporting their staff. Three months after arriving in Australia I had been flown business class to so many places around the globe for training purposes that I had achieved gold Qantas frequent flyer status. I was given the best sales and marketing training that the world had to offer.

I witnessed first-hand how the best of the best formed their marketing strategies. I was trained in the best techniques in customer service. I was mentored and managed by some of the leaders in the world's most successful IT organisations.

All was good for a long time. I was being paid exceedingly well; I had a high profile job selling multi-million-dollar IT services to Optus and Telstra; I had been driving around in Audis and BMWs since my early twenties; and I was able to go wherever I wanted to go on holiday (my husband and I once even chartering a plane to do an aboriginal art tour of the Tiwi Islands).

Then the tech crash came, and life was no longer good. The corporates expected longer and longer hours with more and more responsibility. I ended up commuting on a weekly basis from

Sydney to Kuala Lumpur for a number of months while my husband was commuting on a weekly basis to Tokyo.

This was no longer fun. I had no time for friends or family and I honestly felt that all I was doing was taking lots of money from one large corporate and giving it to another large corporate. In essence, I felt that the job that I was spending such a huge amount of my time doing had no soul. I was burnt out, exhausted, and felt that I had to get out of the rat race for the good of my sanity and my marriage.

So in 2004, after many months of soul searching, I decided that I needed a complete change. I wanted to help people, to make a difference, to give back. So I decided to go back to college and retrain to be a counsellor, NLP practitioner, and clinical hypnotherapist. Yes, I've heard more than a lifetime's worth of 'look into my eyes' jokes!

Because of the amazing amount of training and experience that I received in my corporate life, I found it extremely easy to sell and market myself as a private practitioner. In fact, I had a full practice as soon as I qualified (I had been busy networking with other small businesses throughout my training). I had, of course, started the business with a great website, a beautiful logo, business cards, and brochures, and I was an early adopter of Google Adwords. I had spent as much as I could on my marketing. I was also a prolific networker and understood the importance of word-of-mouth advertising.

Very quickly, people in my industry began to ask why my practice was so busy and needing to refer people on. What was I doing that they weren't? Why had they been in practice for years and only attracted a handful of patients while I had been in practice for a number of months and become fully booked? People started to ask me to meet them for coffee and share with them what I was doing. They then started to ask me to come and talk to their industry and modality groups about what they could be doing differently to attract new patients.

I had an 'aha' moment when I went to a course run by a national psychology association on how to start up and run a practice. I was honestly appalled. It was without doubt the worst training course that I had ever attended. And to top the lot, it was sold out twice over. At that moment, I realised that I could do a much better job and decided to start a business training health professionals to run a successful private practice.

My private practice coaching business went really well. I was running training events, had a networking group, and was providing one-on-one coaching for a select number of allied health professionals. But I knew that there was a missing piece in my offering. I had seen a huge gap in the market for website, design, and marketing services. I tried to partner with a number of companies who could provide these services but there were none that could deliver what my specialised market needed.

I decided to start a family and had two children in quick succession, stopping all my entrepreneurial activity. But after two and a half years of being a stay-at-home mum, I wanted to get myself back into business. A venture that provided websites and marketing services to health, medical, and dental professionals seemed like a great occupation that I could manage while looking after my family.

In 2009, when I launched Wellsites (delivering dental, healthcare, and medical marketing solutions), I had the romantic idea that this business could be a hobby that would grow when the children started school and I was ready to work full time again. Little did I know...

I honestly did not realise how badly the area of health, medical, and dental had been serviced in terms of marketing guidance. My business has grown exponentially from day one, and I am proud to say that we have never cold called to get a client. All enquiries have come to us via our marketing efforts and reputation.

Very early on, we realised that amongst all of our clients our 'sweet spot' was dentists. We find dentists smart, easy to do business with, receptive to new ideas, honest, and decisive. Although we will work with medical and health care specialists, 75% of our services are delivered to the dental industry. In early 2015 we launched My Dental Marketing to reflect this focus in our business.

The longer that I have worked in the dental space, the more opportunities I have seen to help my clients. My Dental Marketing now deliver a wide and constantly expanding range of services including marketing planning and consulting, website design, graphic design, email newsletters, public relations (PR), search engine optimisation (SEO), pay per click (PPC), social media services, marketing campaign programs, and many others. The list is forever growing.

And that is how I've ended up here, ready to deliver the marketing best practice and secrets I've discovered on my journey, so you too can manage your marketing all the way to a full appointment book.

Dental Mgr

- To serve pts
- To serve staff + owner
  - Help people get good quality care
  - Help people have a good experience
    @ the DDS office (not scary)
- Help pts utilize Benefits to best
  meet their needs that wanted
- Help pts get or find ways to
  pay for care where need to but
  seems out of budget.
- Help pts understand what is
  being suggested or recommended
  + why - consequences if don't have done.
- Be a good steward over resources
  of office to serve pts, staff, Dr.
- Continuous look for ways to serve
  Better!

Step 1:
Get Back To Basics

What is your 'why'?

Before I even start talking about marketing your practice, it is important for you to go right back to the beginning and think about why you started your practice in the first place. In essence, what drives you to be where you are today? What is at the core of you doing what you are doing?

> 'People don't buy what you do, they buy why you do it.'
>
> Simon Sinek

- Why did you choose dentistry as your career?
- Why did you risk everything and open a dental practice?
- Why do you continue to work so hard to deliver dental services?
- What does it mean to you and what does that say about you as a person?

What, truly, honestly, is your 'why'? We spend so much time trying to break the code on the 'how' of business success that we often forget about our 'why'.

The 'why' is so important because it is what drives the passion, the soul, and the purpose in your heart and business.

Getting to your 'why'

In his book *Start With Why*, Simon Sinek says, 'People don't buy what you do, they buy why you do it.'

Your friends don't like you for what you do. They like you for who you are. The same is true for patients and employees. Many businesses have lost perspective. They know what they do, but have forgotten the reason.

Do you know why you are in business? Why did you set up and continue to run your practice? Why do you get up everyday to work in your practice? Really, truly, and honestly, do you know your 'why'?

Here are a few questions to ask yourself:

- What does success mean to me?

- What am I most passionate about?

- In what way is my practice an extension of my passion?

- If I could make a difference for anyone or anything, what would it be?

- What are some small steps I can take to begin to make that difference?

- How can I support or contribute to a cause, organisation, individual, or group that stands for something that is important to me?

• Is my passion represented in my practice culture, mission, and vision?

Spend time answering these questions and you will likely find your 'why'. Knowing your purpose may compel you to take on challenges that will stretch you as much as they inspire you.

Identifying your core values

> '*Marketing is really just about sharing your passion.*'
> Michael Hyatt

Too often, short-term planning clouds good business decision-making and causes us to make the wrong move. The only way to meet long-term goals is to root them in missions worthy of our dedication and the kinds of values that meaningfully connect us and enable us to relate deeply to the world around us.

The best companies develop core values that impact their company culture, brand, and business strategies, making them unique.

I believe that when you ask people why they are in business, those with the strongest values are the ones that will continue to grow and flourish.

Incorporating values into recruitment

Hiring staff purely on the basis of their talent and then training them on the values that matter to your company simply doesn't work in the long term. Instead, hiring decisions should focus on issues like character from the start. That way, you'll build a team who innately understand your practice's purpose and will make practical and principled, self-directed decisions day-to-day that put the patient first.

Don't stop there, either. Make sure to reward people not just for getting the job done but for how they get the job done.

Measuring progress based on values

The old adage that 'what you measure is what you get' remains valid.

Not only should you measure 'how much got done' (i.e. profits and losses) but also, more importantly, keep track of 'how it got done'. Patient surveys are a great way to monitor this.

Inspiring your employees

Conventional wisdom tells us that "carrots" are a better motivational tool than "sticks". But even "carrots" have limits, particularly during tough economic times. Instead, leaders need to inspire their employees.

Think about how much we are asking of employees today. We want them to go beyond merely serving patients to create unique, delightful experiences; to honourably represent your practice and nurture its brand, not only when they are on the job but whenever they publicly express; and to be creative with fewer resources and resilient in the face of unimaginable uncertainty.

These contributions will not come as the result of threats or even bonuses. Instead, as a practice owner and leader of your staff, you must inspire your employees with a sense of deep purpose and shared values.

Core values example – Zappos

An example that I love when it comes to a business with great core values is Zappos, the USA-based online shoe store, commonly cited as the world's leading example in customer service:

- Deliver WOW Through Service

- Embrace and Drive Change

- Create Fun and A Little Weirdness

- Be Adventurous, Creative, and Open-Minded

- Pursue Growth and Learning

- Build Open and Honest Relationships With Communication

- Build a Positive Team and Family Spirit

- Do More With Less

- Be Passionate and Determined

- Be Humble

Identifying your ideal patient

One of the cornerstones of any marketing campaign is knowing who your 'ideal patient' is. Many practices make the mistake of avoiding this stage in the eagerness of going ahead with their marketing campaign as soon as possible. You need to stop and think about whom your marketing will be directed to, what they want, what problems they have, and what solutions they need.

The key for implementing a strategic marketing plan is for dentists to identify their practices' ideal patient or target patient profile. Once you know your target market, you need to get to know how best to communicate with them.

Take into consideration what activities will best help reach these people. For example, general dentists, orthodontists, and paediatric dentists might focus on reaching mothers. In this day and age, social media marketing and electronic patient communication would be a better use of the marketing budget to reach that particular demographic than advertising in the Yellow Pages print directory.

For a young demographic, you may turn to the Internet, whereas for an ethnic demographic, you may want to communicate using an ethnic community newspaper.

How to identify your ideal patient

You may find that you have more than one 'ideal patient' (e.g. busy corporate workers and mothers with young children). You will notice by doing this exercise that each type of 'perfect patient' will have different characteristics.

We recommend that you have a different marketing campaign for each one of your ideal patients. Think about:

- Who is your ideal patient?
- Where do they live?
- Where do they work?
- What gender are they?

- What age are they?

- How much do they earn?

- What lifestyle do they have?

- What are their attitudes towards your services?

- What are your ideal patients' issues?

- How do your services help them?

- What do they want to know/what questions do they have about your services?

- What are their concerns and fears about your services?

- What do they read? Who do they talk to? Where do they shop?

- What age groups and ethnicities are most represented?

- What social media platforms do they use?

- How do they want to book an appointment?

- What do they want in terms of location and opening hours?

Another way that you could do this is to look at your existing patients and identify the most profitable. Is there any commonality in terms of demographic and behaviour? You then should think about how you could go about attracting and retaining more of this type of patient.

It is important that this processes is repeated every year to identify any demographic shifts to the economics of your area that you need to be aware of. This is important as demographic shifts could change the demand for the service mix you provide.

Understanding your patients

Marketing starts with identifying your patients' needs and matching them with the skills and services within your practice, ensuring the right team and systems are in place to support this process.

> 'Leverage the strength that you have: that no one else can be you.'
>
> Todd Wheatland

Here are some of the things your target patients may be interested in finding out:

- **What's in it for them?** Make sure something differentiates you as a dental practice. Stand out from your competitors.

- **What do others think?** Dental reviews are vitally important. Today's consumer often looks at several potential service providers before choosing. Their deciding factor isn't always location, price, or a website's colour schematics. It's often based on a quick reputation check.

- **Do patients enjoy an ongoing relationship with the practice?** Continue to provide your patients with health advice and news that matters to them. This can help them remember who you are when it comes time for them to seek out a dentist.

What is important to your patients?

It is critical to understand what is important to your patients. There have been a number of studies in this area.[1]

It has been found that the most important factors that significantly influenced dental patients' perception of service quality were:

1. **Pricing** – the cost of the appointment and/or treatment.

2. **Responsiveness** – the ease of getting an appointment.

3. **Waiting time** – how long they waited.

4. **Patient comfort** – the levels of anxiety experienced, maintenance of comfort and self-respect, and perceived pain.

5. **Perceived professionalism** – whether they felt adequately informed about treatments.

6. **Practice ambience** – their view on the physical characteristics of the practice (decor, equipment, uniforms, marketing material).

You should understand that most of your patients do not have the knowledge to assess your skill or work. They therefore rely on the experiential cues to assess your service quality.

Pricing

The high cost of dental work is a common complaint. Price is central to the patient perception of you and your services. It is all about what your patients consider good or bad value.

Tips to combat poor price perception:

• Build trust by spending time with your patients and demonstrating a genuine interest in them and their health.

- Take the time to clearly and simply inform the patient of all of the treatment options and their associated benefits and risks.

- Encourage frequent visits. The more often you see a patient the greater the opportunity to build your relationship, rapport, and trust.

Responsiveness

Responsiveness is all about a dentist's ability to schedule and keep appointments. Ask yourself:

- How easy is it for patients to schedule an appointment?

- Are you able to fit in patients at short notice?

- Do you offer flexible opening times (early mornings, late evenings, or weekends)?

You also need to think about how easy is it to book appointments with you:

- Do you offer online booking?

- Do you have forms on your website?

- Can they email your practice?

- Is the only way for them to request or book an appointment with you via the phone?

Waiting time

Lack of punctuality is a common patient complaint. Trying to pack as many patients in as you can causes overruns and late appointments. Consider allocating additional time to each patient so that they feel well cared for and not rushed. This can then work as a buffer if any appointments overrun.

Patient comfort

This is about the levels of anxiety experienced, maintenance of patient comfort and self-respect, and perceived pain.

Think about what you are doing to increase the level of comfort for your patients. Here are a few ideas that can make a difference:

- Warm towels at the end of an appointment.
- Blankets over patients' knees during an appointment.
- TV screens to provide distraction.
- A choice of music.
- Noise-cancelling earphones.
- Lip salve.
- Eye masks.

Perceived professionalism

This concerns whether the patient feels adequately informed about treatments. Patients want to feel as though they have been given a choice about what happens to them. Clear communication is key.

Practice ambience

The ambience of the practice concerns everything about the practice's look and feel:

- Physical characteristics of the practice (decor, equipment, uniforms, marketing material).
- Happiness of staff.
- Politeness and helpfulness of staff.

- Televisions or games.

- Children's toys.

- Dental technology.

- Price and ease of parking.

What hours do your ideal patients want you to open?

This is another area of greater and greater importance. We live in an increasingly busy world. People are wanting and expecting increasingly flexible opening hours, be that before or after business working hours or at the weekends. If you are working in a business district area, an absolute must is to be able to see patients early in the morning and later in the evening to fit around people's busy schedules. If you are focusing on families, blocking out times that are just for children in the couple of hours after the end of school could differentiate your practice.

Thinking about your patient demographic and changing the way you run your practice accordingly is key to marketing. Make sure that you communicate changes to your patients.

In summary

You may find that your practice is strong in one or two areas but not across all the aspects that are required for excellent service. A dentist offering next-day treatment for emergencies, supported by caring, empathetic staff is great for service. But if you're running late and operate from a surgery that has seen better days, you have to work harder to overcome those negative impressions.

Knowing your competition

There was a time when the only competition that you had to worry about was the other independent dental practices in the 8km radius around your practice. Nowadays, there has never been

'Marketing is a contest for people's attention.'

Seth Godin

a greater amount of competition and it has never been harder and yet more important to market your dental practice. It has never been more difficult to thrive as a dentist in Australia. There are a number of well-discussed factors affecting how you and your practice are competing:

- **The oversupply of dentists** – Australia will have a dentist glut until at least 2025 as there are too many dentists being trained and registered in Australia (resulting from establishment of new dental schools at regional universities). Plus, the number of overseas trained dentists has increased from fifty to over three hundred over the last four of the last five years[2]. As a consequence there are more and more dental practices opening around the country.

- **The growth of the dental corporates** – There is an increasing trend to corporatisation of the dental industry in Australia in line with the United States. These corporates have aggressive growth plans and are expanding rapidly, buying up increasing numbers of dental practices, hence, increasing competition and driving down dental salaries as they capitalise on the oversupply of dentists. With their impressive marketing strategies and budgets, they are targeting your patients.

- **Preferred providers** – In the past ten years, private health insurance providers have begun aggressively targeting an increase in the numbers of contracted dentists. Medical insurance companies and their preferred provider model are also greatly affecting the competition. They are fixing procedure rates with their preferred providers in your locality or opening up their own dental practices. The insurance companies are targeting your existing patients with the promise of lower priced procedures.

- **Overseas dental providers** – Dental tourism is increasing in popularity. Australian dentists now have to complete against overseas providers. In the current economic climate, many patients consider treatment in Australia to be too expensive and are choosing to travel overseas. Insurance provider NIB is now providing cover for certain procedures to be carried out overseas.

In addition to the above, there are also a number of issues that affect dental practices:

- **Over supply or under-demand?** – A question that has to be asked is whether there is actually an oversupply of dentists or an under-demand. A *Health Workforce Australia* report found a fifth of all adults don't go to a dentist often enough to maintain good oral health.[3] The ADIA have calculated that 23,000 dentists would be needed if everybody went to the dentists once a year. This, in theory, means that the opportunity for the dental profession would be significant if the Australian public were to change their oral hygiene habits.

- **New dental services and offerings** – There are increasing factors contributing to dental practice competition including price positioning (e.g. 'no-gap' offerings) and new service (range and quality, new techniques and technology).

- **Luxury goods** – Fred Joyal, in his book *Everything Is Marketing*, talks at length about how dentistry is a discretionary spend and the real competition to dentistry are the luxury goods providers. Consumers happily spend thousands on a new car, piece of electronic equipment, or holiday and yet the average spend per year on dental work in Australia is $221.[4]

- **Educated consumers** – Your patients and potential patients are getting more and more savvy about where they go to get dental services. They are being bombarded with over six hundred pieces of advertising every day. Their experience of marketing and marketing messaging is getting more sophisticated and their expectations higher.

A word on corporate marketing

Corporate practices bring with them professional marketing support and big marketing budgets. The main focus of their high-impact advertising is to bring new patients through the door. This really raises the bar for the independent practices that want to get noticed.

So how is the corporate approach different from that of an independent practice? First, they have a plan in place that calls for consistent long-term communication. Their objective is to build a recognisable brand that gets stronger month after month and year after year. Second, they have professionally-designed communications that they know will resonate with the patients they're targeting. Finally, they use an integrated approach to cover all the touch points. It's not a scattergun approach.

Independent practices can offer bespoke personalised services that the corporates can never offer. In the coming steps, learn how you can market your differences and strengths, while having a well thought out and strategic marketing plan.

Step 1 – Checklist

	YES	NO
Do you know your 'why'?	O	O
Have you written down your core values?	O	O
Have you articulated your core values to your staff?	O	O
Have you identified your ideal patient?	O	O
Do you know what is important to your patients?	O	O
Do you know your competition?	O	O

Bonus Material

To download checklists and documents that accompany this book:

Go to www.fullybookeddentist.com/resources

Step 2:
Start With A Plan

The importance of having a plan

When it comes to business, Benjamin Franklin's warning, 'By failing to prepare, you are preparing to fail', has never been more apt. Without a marketing plan, how will you know where you are heading and what you are trying to achieve? Without a plan, how will you ever evaluate whether your marketing attempts have been successful?

'A goal without a plan is just a wish.'

Antoine de Saint-Exupéry

I've worked with hundreds of practices, and most dentists don't know what a complete plan looks like or how to implement it if they do have one. This step will guide you through some of the basic elements required in a workable plan for your practice, while the steps to come will explain how to implement in your strategy.

Creating your marketing plan

Good marketing is a marathon, not a sprint. You need a long-term approach. Having a solid marketing plan and systems in place to make it easy to execute it, month after month, is key. You need to have all the basics in place to get results.

How much time should my plan cover?

Make sure you give yourself enough time to succeed. If you don't, you will experience an undercurrent of urgency that will stifle both your creativity and your energy.

Usually, the entire process of creating and implementing an initial marketing plan takes about fifteen months:

- The first three months are dedicated to the planning and creation stage.
- The implementation stage runs for a year.

You should begin the creation stage of the second year's marketing plan three months before the end of the current year's implementation stage, and so on.

Who should create my marketing plan?

An individual dental practice owner may find it difficult to know which marketing efforts will best work for their business. If marketing does not come naturally, a trusted dental marketing consultant or strategic adviser can help guide you. Relying on experts to select the most appropriate and effective marketing mediums to grow the practice may also allow you to focus on what you do best, providing quality dental care to the community.

Whether you are creating your own plan or employing the expertise of dental marketing consultants, identifying your goals, developing a marketing budget and maintaining oversight of the process is crucial.

Setting your goals

Successful practices establish clear short-term and long-term goals before establishing detailed and incremental plans to achieve those goals. Without clear goals, progress and success cannot be measured. What are your goals?

> '*The future you see is the future you get.*'
> Robert G. Allen

The aim of your marketing plan is to achieve the goals set by your business. Critical to your practice success is to have your business, financial, and marketing goals in alignment. The perfect scenario for practice success is when your business coach and marketing coach or consultant works in close collaboration with you.

Identifying your growth needs

The first thing to do is identify your desired growth goals. Most practices fit within three specific growth models:

1. **Rapid Growth** – This is generally for new practices, recently purchased practices, or practices that experience high turnover. The aim is to bring in a lot of new patients quickly.

2. **Sustained Growth** – The majority of practices fit within this category. Growth is important, but not too fast. The goal is about steady, controlled growth.

3. **Patient Retention** – This is for practices who are in the enviable position of not needing new patients and simply want to retain the patients they have.

Setting SMART goals

The key to successful planning is to set goals that are SMART:

- **Specific** – Your goal needs to be well defined and be clear to anyone that has a basic knowledge of the practice.

- **Measurable** – You need to be able to track whether your goal is being achieved.

- **Agreed Upon** – There should be agreement with the staff involved as to what your goal should be.

- **Realistic** – Your goal must be achievable, with regards availability of resources, knowledge, and time.

- **Time-Based** – Your goal should have an element of time, whether it be an established frequency (daily/weekly) or deadline (a certain date).

Example: SMART Goal

To get forty-five new patients by running a promotion for the months of June and July offering free take-home teeth-whitening kits for all new patients.

Knowing your numbers

In order to truly know how your business is going and be able to plan for where you want it to be, you need to track and analyse your practice figures regularly over time. When you know your figures, you are able to identify the causes and effects of changes that occur and make adjustments where necessary. Knowing your numbers can prevent unnecessary stress, panic, and rash decisions from being made.

Additionally, tracking where new patients are coming from and weighing that against money spent on marketing will give you a clear indication of the effectiveness of your marketing efforts, without which you will never know what to continue, repeat, or stop.

More than 60% of dental practices are unaware of their numbers of lapsed patients, more than 40% do not track where new patients are coming from and almost 30% are unaware how many new patients visit their practice each month.[5]

One element integral to your marketing strategy and budget is your calculation of the lifetime value of a patient.

Calculating patient lifetime value

Lifetime value (LV) is a determination of the financial value a patient brings in over their 'lifetime' with your practice. The key to understanding LV lies in the recognition that a patient does not represent a single transaction but a relationship that is far more valuable than any one-time exchange.

However, lifetime value is not about any one patient; it is about stepping back and taking a look at your patient base as a whole. Understanding that, while some never return and some never leave, on average there is a typical patient lifetime and that lifetime has a specific economic value.

> If you don't know what a patient is worth, you don't know what you should plan to spend to get one or what you should plan to spend to keep one.

Determining how much the average new patient spends in your practice over the lifetime of the relationship is crucial to running a successful practice. It enables you to make informed, fact-based decisions about your advertising, including how much you should be willing to spend to acquire a patient, which approaches are actually paying off, and whether you're getting the best return on investment (ROI).

One of the biggest mistakes dental practices make when running their practice numbers is looking only at what a new patient spends in the first visit. Why is this wrong? You'll most likely not do any major treatment on the patient for eighteen to thirty-six months. If you only consider the initial visit, you're overlooking the important, ongoing production that only comes over time, and this will significantly skew your calculations. Marketing expense has to be viewed against the long-term value of the patient.

Step 1

To begin, you need to think about the average timespan that a patient stays with your practice. For most practices, and given the current economic climate, seven years is a conservative number. I have used this in the sample calculation below. Feel free to use your own number if it differs.

Next, what does the average patient spend over that time period? For the purposes of our sample, we'll use a low estimate of $500 a year (assuming some restorative work and regular maintenance).

Again, use whatever average number you think is accurate for your practice. $500 is probably on the low side, especially when you factor in whitening, cosmetic treatment, and implants.

Using these numbers, a single patient is worth $3,500 over their life in the practice.

Example Calculation #1	
Average years in your practice	7
Average amount spent per year	x $500
Value of one patient	$3,500

Step 2

After you've determined the value of one patient, there's a second, more critical part of the calculation (and it's one that most dentists miss): secondary referrals.

If your team is actively asking for referrals, and providing a good dental experience, a typical new patient is estimated to refer five new patients over the next five years. Write in whatever number of referrals you believe to be true for your practice.

That means, if a new patient spends an average of $3,500 and goes on to refer five additional patients (each spending an average of $3,500), that's another $17,500.

Example Calculation #2	
Value of one patient	$3,500
Average number of referrals	x 5
Value of one patient	$17,500

Step 3

You have to consider income from secondary referrals as part of the value of that first patient. After all, you never would have seen them without the initial advertising that attracted them. Now you need to add it all up. The total lifetime value of this sample patient is $21,000.

Example Calculation #3	
Value of one patient	$3,500
Production from referrals	+ $17,500
Value of one patient	$21,000

This $21,000 of production for your practice all stems from a single new patient over a seven-year period. This highlights the importance of not only giving your patients continued great services but also how having an ongoing, active, and publicised referral campaign can have a huge impact on your production.

> 'A budget is telling your money where to go instead of wondering where it went.'
> Dave Ramsey

Setting your marketing budget

Sticking to a predetermined marketing budget and creating a thoughtful plan for implementation will ensure that you are spending your hard-earned money to maximise the reach and return on investment of your marketing efforts.

Setting and adhering to a marketing budget may seem like a daunting task for many dental practitioners, but this is a critical step in implementing a successful practice marketing strategy.

How much should I spend on my marketing?

Marketing is an investment. A dental practice should be spending somewhere between 2-10% of their annual gross income on marketing. This includes planning fees, personnel time, production costs, and implementation costs. Your marketing budget is very much dependant on your business goals:

Rapid Growth	This is generally for new practices, recently purchased practices, or practices that experience high turnover. The goal is to bring in a lot of patients quickly. This is the most expensive because it requires a lot of awareness-marketing.	**Recommendation** **7% – 10%** of your annual gross income.
Sustained Growth	The majority of practices fit within this category. Growth is important, but not too fast. It's really about steady, controlled growth. Sustained growth requires more moderated marketing efforts.	**Recommendation** **4% – 7%** of your annual gross income.
Patient Retention	For practices in the enviable position of not needing new patients and simply wanting to retain the patients they have. This level is all about enhancing the experience of current patients.	**Recommendation** **2% – 3%** of your annual gross income.

Putting aside your monthly budget

Once you have calculated your annual budget, I recommend dividing that number by twelve and putting aside a twelfth of the total each month. If you get in the habit of doing this, you will always have some marketing funds available to ensure a consistent marketing effort.

The most successful dentists are those who are consistent in their marketing efforts. Consistency requires funding, and funding should be carefully planned and budgeted.

Calculating return on investment

Return on investment (ROI) is a simple calculation you can use to evaluate the success of your marketing tactics. In order for you to calculate your marketing return, you need to have systems in place to track the patients and referrals that are generated.

To calculate the ROI for any marketing campaign, you simply divide the dollars you receive by the dollars you invested, using the lifetime value of a patient for a given period of time.

I recommended that you should be trying to get a ROI of 3:1 or above for all your marketing campaigns.

Return on Investment (ROI) example

Let's say a given campaign brought in fifty new patients and cost you $10,000.

You may decide to track your marketing ROI against the two-year value of a patient (of $1,000)

50 new patients x $1,000 average value of a patient = $10,000 invested

$50,000 = 5:1 ROI

$10,000

Any ROI over a 3:1 ratio is good.

Hence, you should keep doing or even do more of this type of marketing in this example.

Implementing your marketing plan

People often get lost at the most important stage of their marketing plan, implementation. It may feel as though, once you've outlined a strategy, you've already done everything at this point, but you haven't. Now that you have done all the hard work, you must actually follow the plan you have invested so much of your time in and see it through to the end. Otherwise, you will lose all of your momentum, not to mention money, time and brain cells.

Nominate someone to be in charge of implementing your plan and to be responsible for staying on time and within budget. It doesn't matter whether that person is external or internal, only that the person has the time and energy to dedicate to your success. Unless you actually set aside time to work on your plan, it will be pushed aside in the daily grind and forgotten. Then you will have lost your investment, because the key to a successful marketing plan is consistency and repetition, fuelled by enthusiasm. If you work your plan only sporadically or at the last minute, then you lose the awareness you are building.

Planning for a marathon, not a sprint

Once the marketing strategies have been determined, put them into a calendar or timeline to ensure that those who have been tasked with the responsibility can execute the plan.

Careful thought should be given to the timing of each activity, and marketing activities should be scheduled and spread throughout the entire year, with focus given to the slower times of the year when prospective patients aren't necessarily looking for dental care.

Tracking your plan

Tracking is perhaps the most essential aspect of your marketing. Without it you're shooting, or rather spending, in the dark. You have to know in detail how many patients each type of advertising is generating. This can easily be done within your practice management software. Virtually all practice management software programs have a place to enter 'referral source', and most will run a variety of reports that will tell you exactly how your advertising is working.

Half the money I spend on advertising is wasted; the trouble is I don't know which half.

John Wanamaker

If a certain strategy does not yield acceptable results, it does not necessarily indicate that the idea was a complete failure. Sometimes simple tweaks can produce improved results.

Case study

The importance of knowing your numbers is constantly brought home to me when I talk to practices who have existing Google Adwords (or Pay Per Click) campaigns. These campaigns, if not tracked and managed well, can be a large hole in which to tip your money.

I was recently talking to a general dental practice in a suburb outside of Melbourne. This practice had been spending $7,000 a month for a period of nearly two years. They wanted to know if I thought that they were getting a good return on investment.

I asked them if they had been tracking where their new patients had been coming from and luckily they had. When they ran the report, we found out that they had been attracting fifty-two new patients a month on average over the last six months. Of these, forty had been word of mouth and twelve were found 'online'.

Even if 100% of the new 'online' patients had come from their Google Adwords campaign, this still meant that they were paying $583 for every new patient this way.

We then looked at the Google Adwords and found out that 97% of their Google Adwords spend had been targeting keywords for the whole of Melbourne. They had been spending $7,000 a month to get a click on an advert by a majority of people that were located nowhere near their practice.

We worked with them to change their Google Adwords set-up, reduce their spend, and increase the number of patients coming to their practice via Google.

If this practice had known their numbers and had been looking at them months (or even years) before, how much wasted money could they have spent on better campaigns and how many more patients could they now have been treating?

Step 2 – Checklist

	YES	NO
Do you know the growth needs of your practice?	○	○
Have you set SMART goals?	○	○
Have you calculated your patient lifetime value?	○	○
Have you set your marketing budget?	○	○
Are you putting aside your monthly marketing budget?	○	○
Have you set processes in place to track your marketing return on investment?	○	○

Bonus Material

To download checklists and documents
that accompany this book:

Go to www.fullybookeddentist.com/resources

Step 3: Build The Right Foundation

Building a great team

Building and maintaining a great dental team is one of the most important components of your practice marketing. The bottom line is that an experienced and well-informed dental team goes a long way to maintaining a happy practice environment and contented patients.

'Never forget that you only have one opportunity to make a first impression.'

Natalie Massenet

What your patients experience when coming to your practice is based on the attitude and approach of your staff. If they see happy, satisfied staff, then they're likely to be contented and satisfied patients.

Once you've hired the right team, you should focus on consistently looking after your team members by:

• Training staff to keep their clinical, business and soft skills up to date.

• Listening to your staff in regular and structured staff meetings.

- Showing gratitude to your staff, enhancing employee loyalty and commitment.

Successful business leaders recruit, train, and lead productive, principled, and passionate teams.

Appointing a marketing coordinator

Many practices struggle to implement effective marketing programs because they lack the necessary manpower. Dentists often take on this role and fail because they simply do not have time to maintain a consistent, long-term, internal marketing program.

Marketing should be the responsibility of a marketing coordinator. This is a team member who can dedicate a number of hours to creating and implementing the appropriate strategies. With the dentist seeing patients all day, he or she doesn't have the time to also successfully promote the practice. This position is incredibly important, as most marketing programs cannot reach their full potential without one. Practices need to use a minimum of ten ongoing marketing strategies; to do this successfully, there needs to be a marketing coordinator.

Your marketing coordinator will work with your marketing coach or consultant and should handle 90% of the marketing program, with other staff members participating on a patient-by-patient basis.

Preparing your team

Preparation is all about communication. Marketing campaigns are more successful if your entire team is aware of each program's goals and what's involved in each initiative.

Ensure everyone knows what marketing campaigns are running. They should understand and be able to articulate what makes your practice different and its key attributes. Your entire staff should be able to respond to questions about your practice accurately and confidently.

It takes time to build marketing awareness and it will be a team effort, but this will have a significant impact on response. Encourage existing patients and team members to take promotional offers and referral cards to hand out to family, friends, and to local business owners. Thank everyone for their support.

Creating the right first impression

Interpersonal relations

Believe it or not, marketing begins with interpersonal relations. I have seen many practices attempt to implement marketing strategies, only to be thwarted at every turn because the dental team lacked sufficient interpersonal skills. One of the first areas that should be addressed before implementing any marketing campaigns is training the team in interpersonal skills.

81% of patients come to a dental practice by word-of-mouth referral, however, 85% of your patients will leave you for what they perceive is a lack of patient service.[6]

If the team lacks sufficient verbal and interpersonal skills, they will provide average patient service and will probably not build strong relationships with patients. If this is the case then any attempts at carrying out successful marketing will likely fail.

I recommend that you assess your team from an interpersonal relations standpoint. This includes evaluating:

- How the phone is answered.

- How patients are greeted.

- How often assistants check in with patients to see if they are comfortable during procedures.

- What your assistants say to patients when the dentist leaves the treatment room.

- The way that hygienists relate to and educate patients.

- How the front desk personnel interact with patients during check-in and checkout.

- How new patients are treated during orientation and the initial consultation.

- How your team is presenting and communicating treatment options to your patients. Is this done in a way to enable your patients to make informed decisions while building trust and long lasting relationships?

Many people do not naturally have exceptional interpersonal skills. This is not an area generally taught as part of their training. You may hire staff with amazing technical skills but if their personal skills are not up to scratch then they may not have the skills to necessarily relate to their patients in a positive way.

I recommend that you seriously consider investing in some interpersonal training. There are some incredible courses available that specifically cater for the dental industry. (See Resources for more information.)

Building the right image

Your practice brand

Branding is an extremely important aspect of your practice. An effective brand strategy helps you to differentiate yourself from your competition, to stand out from the crowd, and to articulate your values. Your practice brand is what you communicate visually and verbally to your patients and community

To build and maintain a strong brand, you will need to be consistent in your branding in every point of contact customers have with you.

Key elements of your brand

Every possible contact and piece of communication with a patient or potential patient should reinforce your brand. The main elements that make up your practice brand are:

- Your business name
- Any slogans or taglines you use
- Your logo
- Your premises
- How you and your employees dress
- Your practice website
- The style and quality of your practice stationery – business cards, brochures, etc.
- Where and how you advertise

Developing a brand personality

Businesses, like people, have distinct personalities that create customer experiences. A set of human characteristics can be attributed to a brand and this is known as the brand personality.

Your brand personality is something to which your patients can relate. An effective brand will increase its brand equity by having a consistent set of traits. This is the added-value that a brand gains, aside from its functional benefits.

Think about your practice as a person and what personality traits it would exhibit, such as caring, fun, rule breaking, understanding, expert, independent, etc. Then look at your logo, your tag line, and the language that you use in marketing your practice and see if these are all in line with your brand personality.

There is a whole branch of branding called brand archetypes (that I find fascinating) which goes into brand personalities in much more depth (beyond the scope of this book). I recommend that you look into brand archetypes if you want to dig deeply into your brand personality.

The importance of your logo

The foundation of your brand is your logo and it is a critical aspect of your practice marketing. Your logo design establishes your identity. A logo is intended to be the 'face' of a company and is your practice's major graphical representation. A logo anchors a practice's brand and becomes the single most visible manifestation of your practice. For this reason, a well-designed logo is an essential part of your overall marketing strategy.

A logo provides essential information about a company that allows customers to identify with the company's core brand. It is a shorthand way of referring to your practice in advertising and marketing materials. It also provides an anchor point for the various fonts, colours, and design choices in all other business-marketing materials.

Having just any logo, however, is not enough to create a brand identity for you. A badly thought up logo can very easily destroy the image of your practice. On the other hand, a carefully designed logo can reach the public and communicate to them the worth of your practice. Therefore, so much depends on the design of your logo.

So invest the time and budget in developing a great logo for your practice.

The importance of brand consistency

Your branding elements should be consistent and repeated throughout all of your communication with your patients.

If all these are consistently in line with your brand values, your brand will be strengthened. But if they are not in line, your brand, and your business, could be seriously damaged. A brand makes promises to customers and if they aren't fulfilled, your customers will be far less likely to buy again.

The deadly sins of dental branding

I feel that any book on dental marketing and any section on branding needs to have something said about the importance of a great logo and the mistakes that I see. I apologise in advance if what I am about to say upsets you, but I feel that it needs to be reinforced.

The days of having a logo that is a clip art image of a happy tooth holding a toothbrush are over. You cannot do this. You can no longer 'build your own' and you cannot 'steal' an image from another practice's logo and add your own practice name. Yes, I have seen all of this and many more logo deadly sins in my time.

You have to remember that patients are savvier than ever before. They are constantly exposed to a huge amount of branding. Their expectations of what is and is not professional are increasing. The reality is that when you are competing against the corporates, you need to ensure that your branding is up to scratch.

It is also very common for practices to have their branding and logo professionally designed and then decide to 'take it over', producing homemade brochures and other marketing collateral that use different colours, fonts, and even different versions of the logo. They often use free templates or tools not meant for design work (such as using Microsoft Word to produce a practice brochure).

I understand that practices are trying to save time and money by doing this, but the result gives your practice an unprofessional feel. If you are not consistent, your attempts at establishing a brand will be damaged.

Branding summary

Branding takes time to pass on from you to your staff, from your staff to your patients, and from your patients to other potential patients and into the community. Stay disciplined. Keep supporting your brand idea. Let it slowly and steadily seep into the community. Branding success happens slowly, not all at once. Persistence pays off.

Your practice appearance

One significant part of marketing is the appearance of your practice. In patients' minds, a modern practice's appearance indicates modern standards of hygiene, sterility, and how up-to-date the practice is with the latest procedures, techniques, and materials.

Both you and your staff should carry out an exercise to look at your practice 'through the eyes of a patient'. Too many dental practices do not notice a gradual decline in the appearance of their facility. Many times I have been into a practice and seen old upholstery, a dying pot plant in the corner, magazines in the waiting room that are years old, or old, chipped paintwork.

Do you regularly get new magazines in your practice and throw away the old? Do you have fresh flowers delivered on a weekly basis? How faded are your external signs? How is your paintwork and furniture looking? A simple coat of paint and regular changes of the furniture (or even new cushions) in the waiting room every few years can do wonders.

Lifting the appearance of the practice doesn't need to cost a lot of money.

Knowing your marketing touch points

Dropping the scattergun approach

I speak to many dentists who tell me that they have tried many types of different marketing and they have all failed and 'nothing works for them'. When I dig deeper, I discover that they have tried many different approaches, but nearly all of these have been done in a haphazard way and in short bursts. I call this a scattergun approach to marketing.

It doesn't work to try one approach for a month or two in an inconsistent manner without tracking the results or refining a campaign. This will end in failure.

What are your marketing touch points?

It has been shown that it can take between six to eleven times for patients to see or hear a message before they act on it.[7] Do you know how many ways and how many times you are communicating with your patients?

'Don't put all your eggs in one basket' goes the old saying. As I discussed in the introduction, there is no silver bullet when it comes to marketing. It is important that you see your practice marketing as a collation of strategies. Creating effective marketing with different patient touch points is key to your success. Your potential patients and existing patients need to experience a number of touch points all reinforcing your brand message before making the decision to come to you.

What exactly is a patient touch point?

Patient touch points are your points of patient contact, from start to finish. They embody the interaction of your brand and service with patients, potential patients, and other interested parties. Points of contact occur before a patient decides to use your services, while being treated in your practice, when they pay, and potentially for years afterwards.

At a touch point, a mental and emotional impression is formed. It is the job of every dental team to manage those touch point impressions. Every touch point needs to be well thought out.

Finding your patient touch points

There are hundreds of touch points in the typical dental practice. Identify your patient touch points by making a list of all the places and times your patients might come into contact with your practice brand. The list below is a good place to start:

Influencing Touch Points	The Pre-Purchase Experience	The Purchase Experience	The Post-Purchase Experience
Word of mouth	Advertising	Building exterior	Thank you card
Reviews and ratings	Appointment-making interaction	Receptionist	Follow-up call
Social media	PR	Office surroundings	Online bill payment
Referrals	Website	Parking	Billing statement
	Blog	Examination room	Marketing emails
	Phone calls	Employee uniform	
	Promotions	Staff welcome	
	Online videos	Signage	
	Community involvement		

Example: Patient touch points

This is an example of the process people could go through when looking for a new dentist, coming into contact with the above touch points:

1. Influencing touch points

- They ask friends for recommendations.
- They look at the practice's Facebook page.
- They check out some trusted review websites (for example, Yelp, Google+) for patient ratings and testimonials.
- They remember seeing a local dentist on the news commenting on a new dental procedure.

2. The pre-purchase experience

- They check out the website pages of some of the dentists that have piqued their interest.

- They decide to call one and are thrilled with how pleasant the receptionist is and how quickly they are able to come in for an appointment.

3. The purchase experience

- They arrive at the dentist's office and are greeted by the smiling receptionist. The receptionist is dressed in a uniform with the practice logo on it.

- They sit in the nicely decorated and comfortable waiting room before seeing the dentist.

- The dentist is warm and approachable; they are made to feel relaxed and comfortable and all of their questions are answered.

- On the way out, they stop at the reception desk to pay. The receptionist is smiling and friendly and is able to answer any further questions that they have.

4. The post-purchase experience

- The office staff sends them home with a card containing useful information.

- On the card, they see the dentist's blog and social media pages, which offer dental hygiene tips.

- Someone from the staff calls after their appointment to check on them.

- A couple of days later, they receive a handwritten card with a small token of appreciation for becoming a new patient.

- They go to a ratings website and share their experience with others.

Using your touch points to gather patient feedback

Knowing your touch points is only half the battle. To improve patient satisfaction, you need to make sure each touch point leads to a good patient experience, and that the experience as a whole delivers on patients' expectations.

To see what's working, you can run patient feedback surveys at each major touch point. But make sure not to lose sight of the big picture; always look at your entire patient experience.

> All touch points are not created equal. Some will naturally play a larger role in determining your company's overall patient experience.

Stepping into your patients' shoes is an exercise too many practices neglect when marketing. We forget to become our own patients, with real, day-to-day concerns, and in the process, we lose sight of the most valuable touch point opportunities. Each one is a chance to present your practice and practice brand and what you stand for.

Selecting the right types of marketing

You may not be aware of the fact that you are marketing in different ways to achieve different goals and to attract different types of patients. It is important to understand that there are two types of marketing: internal and external.

Internal marketing

This is the marketing that you do to keep your existing patients and reactivate dormant patients. Internal marketing is how you communicate with your existing patients on every front; it is what you and your staff do after a patient calls you.

Internal marketing is critical as it is everything you do to make certain that the patient remains with your practice.

Examples of internal marketing include:

- The reception area
- Referral brochures
- Wall art
- Phone communication
- Recalls
- Email newsletters
- Patient satisfaction surveys
- Patient 'thank you's
- Rewards programs for loyal patients
- On-hold marketing

External marketing

External marketing is what you do to attract new patients into your practice and entice a patient to contact you.

Examples of external marketing include:

- Print advertising

- Digital advertising

- Website content

- Blogging

- Social media marketing

- Direct marketing

- Practice marketing materials, including logo, business cards, letterhead, and brochures

- Radio & TV commercials

- Yellow Pages advertisements

What marketing is best?

So where do you start? Which type of marketing is best for you and your practice? Which is more important, internal marketing or external marketing?

Many people believe that one size fits all when it comes to marketing. A common perception is that your practice should be doing what their competitors are doing and that all types of marketing are suitable for all types of practices.

You need to think about what you are trying to achieve, who you are trying to market to, and what you want people to do when they see/ hear a particular piece of marketing.

Once again, this comes down to knowing your goals:

- Are you trying to attract new patients to your practice?

- Are you trying to reactivate your existing patients?

- Are you trying to get referrals?

Most likely, you need to have a combination of both types of marketing within your practice. A common mistake that I see when talking to dentists is that they are focused solely on external marketing and trying to get new patients, overlooking the huge value that can be achieved in utilising internal marketing.

Testimonials

I want to offer a word of warning about the use of testimonials in Australia. By testimonial, I mean a 'positive statement about a person or thing'. These can be written statements or videos given to you by your patients.

If you read anything from the USA on marketing, they will talk endlessly about the amazing power of using patient testimonials on all of your marketing. Unfortunately (at the time of writing), practitioners in Australia are unable to use patient testimonials in any form or promotion or advertising. This is due to the guidelines given by Australian Health Practitioner Regulation Agency (AHPRA guidelines), which state:

1. You cannot use or quote testimonials on a website or in social media that is advertising a regulated health service, including patients posting comments about a practitioner on the practitioner's business website.

2. You cannot use testimonials in advertising a regulated health service to promote a practitioner or service.

You will find more information on the AHPRA guidelines in the Resources section at the back of the book.

The ban on using testimonials means it is not acceptable to use testimonials in your own advertising, such as on your Facebook page, in a print, radio, or television advertisement, or on your website.

In summary

At the foundation of your business, you need to have a great team, a strong brand, and a firm understanding of your patient touch points and the different types of marketing. This is the launch point for all of your marketing efforts and practice success to come.

Case study

I was recently asked to talk to a dental practice who needed help with their marketing. One of the first questions I always ask is what existing marketing they had in place. What I heard was a very typical story.

They had a website that had been bought by the previous owner and no longer reflected the team or services they offered. On top of this, the website company had gone out of business and they could not change the content or design.

They had a social media presence and were paying the wife of one of their patients to 'keep their social media happening'. They were paying $500 a month for this service and had been doing so for four months.

They had employed a South African based company to work on their SEO and were paying them $750 a month for this service but didn't know what they were doing or if it was working as they got little or no reporting back from them (and when they did get something, they didn't understand it).

They were also paying $3000 a month for a Google Adwords campaign with yet another company but weren't sure what location or keywords it was targeting. They also weren't tracking to see what their conversions were.

They had also run a few unsuccessful Groupon campaigns, done a letterbox drop, and had sent out two email newsletters in the last year.

This was a true example of a scattergun approach to marketing. And this is, unfortunately, a very common story. When I asked them what their strategy was, what goals they had, and what measurements and targets they had in place for each of the areas – they had none.

We worked with this practice to identify and rate all of their current patient touch points. We looked at where the gaps and priorities were, agreed upon their internal and external marketing strategies, **and, above all, identified what goals they were trying to achieve and how they would track and measure them.**

Step 3 – Checklist

	YES	NO
Do you have a marketing coordinator?	○	○
Is your team briefed and ready for your next steps in marketing?	○	○
Have you assessed your team's interpersonal skills?	○	○
Does your logo and brand reflect you and your practice?	○	○
Have you assessed your practice appearance?	○	○
Is your branding consistent?	○	○
Have you identified all of your marketing touch points?	○	○
Do you know the difference between internal and external marketing and how this relates to your practice?	○	○

Bonus Material

To download checklists and documents that accompany this book:

Go to www.fullybookeddentist.com/resources

Step 4:
Attract The Right Patients

On average, you will lose between 15% to 20% of patients year on year,[8] so it is a critical part of your marketing strategy to attract new patients to your practice. However, while most practitioners focus on getting new patients into their practice, very few know how to effectively attract the right kind of patients. You've identified your ideal patient; now's the time to bring them in with the right kind of external marketing.

> *The challenge for small business is knowing where customers are and reaching them effectively.*
>
> Brad D. Smith

Some dentists shy away from external marketing due to the expense. They see it as big financial risk. However, the most marketing savvy (and highly successful) practices understand that the external marketing budget is an investment in the practice. You can have an explosive ROI when it's managed well.

Addressing frequency versus reach

A critical principle when looking at your external marketing is the concept of frequency versus reach.

Reach and frequency are terms generally used when planning advertising campaigns. However, the principle applies to any promotional activity you undertake: direct mail, online advertising, even networking.

At the heart of the concept is a question: Is it more effective to touch a hundred potential patients once, or twenty-five potential patients four times?

Reach

The number of people you touch with your marketing message who work or live close enough to your practice to respond and make an appointment. For most dental practitioners in suburban/metro settings, this area is rarely larger than a five-to-eight kilometre radius around your practice.

Frequency

The number of times you "touch" each person with your marketing message.

In a world of unlimited resources, you would obviously maximise both reach and frequency. However, as most practices have a limited budget, you will often make decisions to sacrifice reach for frequency or vice versa.

In his book *Permission Marketing*, Seth Godin uses an analogy of seeds and water to demonstrate the importance of assuring adequate frequency in your promotional campaigns.

'If you were given a hundred seeds with enough water to water each seed once, would you plant all hundred seeds and water each

one once, or would you be more successful if you planted twenty-five seeds and used all of the water on those twenty-five seeds?'

One of the biggest wastes of marketing dollars is promotional activity that is implemented without adequate frequency. When faced with the decision, always opt for less reach and more frequency.

When faced with decisions of reach vs. frequency, remember this rule:

Reach without frequency is wasted money

Creating your external marketing message

Your external marketing is directed at prospective new patients who do not know you. You need, therefore, to create a consistent marketing message for use in your external communications that takes this into account.

It starts with knowing the wants, fears, problems, and needs of your target market and ends with crafting a message that speaks to those issues in a compelling and believable way. The result is an irresistible hook that makes your prospect want to know more.

Many practices are confused about their marketing message. Some think it's their slogan and others think it's a regurgitation of all their awards and how long they've been in business. Still others think it's their vision and mission statement. It's none of the above.

The biggest marketing message mistake that practices make is talking about themselves and not about their patients.

Your marketing message is what grabs your ideal patient's attention, tells them how you can solve their problem, why they should trust you, and why they should choose to come to your practice over and above any and all other choices they might have.

Your marketing message should 'speak' to your ideal patient. You need to appeal to your ideal patient's 'hot buttons'. Talk about the areas that will trigger an emotional reaction.

The steps to go through to create your message are as follows:

1. Identify your target market

The first step starts out by asking, 'Who is my target market?' Refer back to your ideal patient profile. Your marketing message needs to be written to this target demographic.

2. Identify the problems your target market experiences

Ask yourself, 'What problem does my target market have and how does it make them feel?'

You need to understand the experiences of your patients to identify their problems and the pain and suffering they feel as a result of those problems. What does your ideal patient want from a dentist? What do they care about? What do they worry about? What is stopping them from coming to a dentist on a regular basis?

Remember the old saying, 'People don't care about you until they know you care'. Making it your mission to identify your market's concerns tells them that you understand and empathise with them.

Examples:

- They are afraid of dental fees.

- They need dental services that work around their office day.

3. Present your services to your market's problem

Ask yourself, 'What do I offer that solves the problems of my ideal patient?'

It is very tempting to talk about your services, e.g. teeth whitening, crowns, etc. But you need to present your practice in terms of solving people's problems.

Examples:

- They are afraid of dental fees – Say that you are fully transparent with your pricing and they can see pricing on your website.

- They need dental services that work around their office day – Say that you offer early morning and late night dental services that work around their office day.

4. Identify the benefits of your services

Now, identify all the benefits of your services and how those benefits could impact your ideal patient.

Examples:

- They are afraid of dental fees – There are never any nasty surprises.

- They need dental services that work around their office day – They don't have to miss work or schedule their appointments around their busy work commitments.

5. Explain what makes you different from your competitors

Ask yourself, 'How am I different from my competitors?'

Potential patients are looking for you to communicate your differences. And those differences need to have perceived value to the prospect. They need to be things they care about.

Do this in such a way as to explain what you stand for and what you can do rather than a direct statement, such as 'We are better than 123 Dental because...'

How does your website measure up?

Having a website working to your advantage is critical in this day and age. Your website is the centre of your marketing hub and should be used as a key component to both your external and internal marketing.

But don't take my word for it; ask yourself and the people in your practice. In the last few years, when have you been told about a new product or service and not gone to look at their website? Think about how you reacted if the website wasn't easy to navigate and didn't quickly and clearly articulate what was on offer.

Many dentists don't know how to promote their website and many dental websites are poorly designed and executed. Your dental practice website needs to educate, promote offers and improve the image of your practice.

So often we speak to practices that have spent or are spending a huge amount of time, money, and effort marketing and promoting their services. They may be spending money on a huge Google Adwords campaign, trying out radio advertising, and investing in a multitude of prints ads. They come to us trying to work out why all of this time and money they are spending is not converting into enquiries and ultimately into bookings.

When we start looking into these problems, we discover the issue is that their website just isn't up to scratch. However you are marketing your practice, a large percentage of people will view your website in order to find out more about you. If they like what they see, they will ultimately contact you.

But what if your website isn't up to scratch? What if it doesn't live up to their expectations? What if they can't easily navigate around your website? All the time, money, and effort that you have just spent marketing could potentially be wasted.

In short, a good website builds credibility. A less-than-professional website is almost worse than nothing.

When you are building or reviewing your website, there are a number of key areas that you need to address to make your website perform:

Know the purpose of your website

You have a website because everyone said you needed one, but you're not really sure what it does. If you don't know, how can your patients know what the purpose of your website is?

You need to have a goal for your website and give it a purpose. What do you want visitors to your website to do? What should your website accomplish? If your website is simply out there to 'provide information' then you have lost significant opportunities.

Your very first step should be to define the goals of your website. Most practices should have at least three or four.

Example goals are:

- To create an online presence.

- To differentiate your business.

- To capture leads.

- To provide information about your practice and services.

Grab visitors' attention before they move onto your competitor's website

More often than not, your homepage will be the initial point of contact with your patients. And you have between three and five seconds to capture their attention before they click away.

Most probably they will land on your website's home page to start with. A good homepage will answer the questions:

- What do you do?

- Why should I trust you?

Visitors will make a split-second decision on whether they will stay to learn more or go to one of your competitors, so don't lose them at the start.

Make it easy to navigate

Website navigation is the most important aspect to consider when designing a website. The primary aim for effective navigation is to keep your visitors in your site, so they find what they're looking for easily and quickly.

How quickly can users locate a particular page on your site? If it takes more than two or three clicks, you may have to reconsider your website layout.

Have call to action buttons

A call to action (CTA) is the button, link, or text on your website that encourages users to take a next step. Some examples of website CTAs might read: 'Book Now', 'Contact Us', 'Sign Up Today', or 'Download a Free eBook'.

CTAs can have a deep impact on your online success. Think about the purpose or goal behind your website. To achieve your goals, you must point visitors in the right direction. Adding thoughtfully designed and carefully placed call to action buttons on your website can cause a higher percentage of visitors to find out more about you, complete a sign up form, or contact you.

Capture leads

It is really important that you capture visitors' details when they visit your website.

Getting prospective patients to sign up to your email list means that you can contact them and no longer have to wait for them to come to you. You can present your special offers and keep them up to date on new services or changes. Email marketing is a really effective way to generate interest in your practice.

Structure your content

How your content is structured on your website is critical to getting people to stay there. Did you know that people rarely read website pages word by word, they scan the page.

This means the content of your website needs to be structured in such a way as to enable scanning. To do this you should:

- Use headings to break text into separate topics.
- Use meaningful sub-headings – questions often make great headings.
- Use bulleted lists.
- Highlight keywords – hypertext links serve as one form of highlighting while typeface variations and colour are others.
- Have one idea per paragraph.
- Bold the first sentence to capture attention.
- Start all pages/articles with the conclusion at the beginning.
- Use short paragraphs of fifty words or less.
- Try to say what you need in the shortest and clearest possible way.
- Have three to five hundred words per page.

Use relevant images

Photos, charts, and graphs are worth a thousand words. Using visuals effectively can enhance readability when they replace or reinforce long blocks of textual content.

A website is a reflection or extension of your physical business. It represents you, your team, and your mission. Your website should give your potential patients the same feelings and emotions that they would have walking into your practice.

Potential patients want to see who you are and what your office looks like before they book an appointment. Your brand, your philosophy, and your dental style need to be conveyed in the first few seconds that a visitor spends on your website. Your website development team will take care of portraying your philosophy and branding, and to make this happen you need to have real photographs.

A study carried out by the Neilson Group showed that users pay 'close attention to photographs and other images that contain relevant information'.[9] Users will, however, ignore certain images, particularly stock photographs, that are merely included as decorative artwork.

What you can do:

- Make sure images you use aid or support textual content.
- Avoid overuse of stock photos and meaningless visuals.

Every website is unique and should have plenty of space to accommodate personal pictures. Take some photographs of your office and your staff or, better still, hire a professional photographer to help you showcase your practice professionally.

Is your website mobile ready?

Anybody who has been on a bus, on a train, or in a cafe in the last few years will realise that the world is now living on his or her mobile phone. According to Forbes, '87% of connected devices sales by 2017 will be tablets and smartphones'.[10]

A staggering 70% of Australians own either a smartphone or tablet device, and 32% own both. The usage statistics indicate that the majority of Australians are highly dependent on their mobile devices; they rarely leave these devices out of hand even in the home.[11]

Due to this widespread (and quickly growing) use of smartphones and tablets, it is necessary for practices to create content that's accessible to mobile users. It is important to provide a positive experience to users that are browsing via a mobile device.

50% of people, even if they like a business, will use them less often if the website isn't mobile-friendly.[12]

- When people visit a mobile-friendly website, 74% of people are more likely to return to that website in the future.

- 67% of mobile users that visit a mobile-friendly website are more likely to buy a website's product or service.

- 30% of Google Ads are accessed by mobile phones. Therefore, if you are using Google Ads and you don't have a mobile website then you are instantly wasting 30% of your money.

If your website is not mobile ready, you may easily lose patients to competitors who have adapted to this trend. As the shift from traditional PCs and laptops to mobile devices continues, businesses that are not mobile ready are likely to suffer.

Responsive website design

As of April 2015, any website that is not mobile-friendly will be penalised by Google.

A mobile-friendly website can be obtained either by creating an alternative mobile version of a website or utilising responsive website design.

I always recommend responsive website design. Having a separate website is a lot of unnecessary administration. The responsive website design approach builds a single website that provides an optimal viewing experience (easy reading and navigation with a minimum of resizing, panning, and scrolling) across a wide range of devices, from mobile phones to desktop computer monitors.

The advantages of a mobile friendly website

The main benefits are speed and ease of use. Although smart phones already allow for website connectivity, creating a mobile version of your website will:

- Provide faster functionality.

- Allow greater connectivity with your patients.

- Bypass geographic restrictions.

By providing visitors with the easiest possible access to your practice, you will increase your chance of an enquiry and gain an edge over your competitors.

Online bookings

I am seeing more and more demand for people to be able to book appointments online. It is a trend that you need to embrace if you want to keep up with your competition. People are more time poor than ever and they are now expecting to be able to contact you and book appointments at a time that is convenient to them. This is probably not going to be at a time when you necessarily have somebody sitting at your reception desk to take their call.

You need to provide as many ways as possible to allow people to contact you. At a minimum you should include the following ways to contact you on your website:

- Phone number.
- Email address.
- Contact form.

Then you should consider online booking systems such as practice management software, online portals, and appointment request forms.

Search marketing – SEO and PPC

It is no use having a great website if nobody can find you online. Your website serves as a virtual extension to your practice, educating and attracting patients who may not have heard of you so far. A major aspect of any brand's online presence is where and how it appears on Google search results.

Where your website appears on Google can have a huge impact on the amount of traffic you receive and consequently, the number of interested patients knocking on your door.

Know the terms – SEO, SEM, PPC

Search engine optimisation and search engine marketing can be a confusing concept to grasp. Often, when I talk to my clients about their search engine marketing strategies, I find that there is a large amount of confusion about what all of the terms mean.

Below are some brief explanations for the terms used in search marketing:

Pay per click (PPC)

Pay per click (sometimes also referred to as search engine marketing (SEM)) is the paid approach to Internet marketing. This is when you pay a certain amount for every click you receive through a search engine. Your ad will appear in the 'Sponsored Results' section of the listing page. With PPC, your rankings will be determined by the amount you bid on keywords and the click-through rate generated by your ads.

Search engine optimisation (SEO)

Search engine optimisation (sometimes also referred to as organic search marketing) is when you modify or improve your website and online presence to rank higher in the organic (regular) listings on

Google, Yahoo, Bing, etc. With SEO, such things as link popularity
and content relevance will determine your rankings.

Pay per click advertising (PPC)

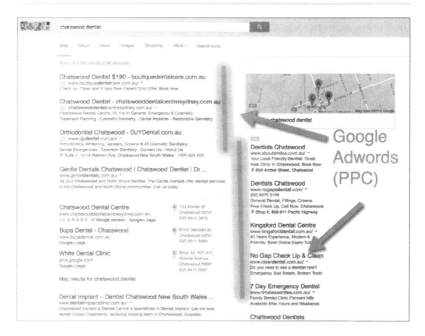

Essentially, pay per click is advertising that appears in search
engine results, on websites, and on social media platforms that
directs visitors to your website. The largest PPC platform is Google's
Adwords, followed by Facebook, LinkedIn, and Bing.

Unlike many other forms of advertising, every cent spent on PPC
advertising can be thoroughly measured and analysed. The great
thing about PPC is that you only pay when someone 'clicks' on your

advertisement, unlike advertising in a newspaper where you pay for the ad upfront irrespective of the results generated.

When should I use pay per click?

Most practices can greatly benefit from pay per click advertising in attracting new patients, if it is done correctly. If you are looking for fast ways to attract patients then PPC should be considered for your dental marketing plan.

How to use pay per click successfully

Pay per click isn't difficult, but it does take time to understand and requires serious effort in planning and executing campaigns.

The key to a successful PPC marketing campaign is in the management of the following elements:

- **Pick the keywords wisely** – Really think about the services that you wish to promote, and hence the keywords you want to select. Do not get pulled into the mistake of picking every keyword associated with dentistry, as this will chew up your budget quickly.

- **Think about your location keywords** – A common mistake I see is that PPC campaigns use a large location term, e.g. advertising for 'teeth whitening Sydney'. Remember that dentistry is a location-based business and unless you are a specialised practice, people will not travel from the other side of the city to see you. Instead use the suburb in which your practice is located and surrounding suburbs.

- **Have campaigns that target specific key words** – Create ad groups that have a specific theme. The goal should be to have ad copy that is relevant to those keywords alone.

- **Use negative keywords** – Add negative keywords and prevent your ads from showing on queries you don't want. E.g. if you are a high-end practice then you should have 'cheap', 'affordable', and 'public' as your negative keywords.

- **Have a strong call to action in your advert** – This will greatly impact the success of your campaign You need to give people a compelling reason to click through your ad.

- **Optimise your landing page** – Have your advert click through to a specific page of your website that talks about the services in your advert (e.g. cosmetic dentistry or emergency treatments). Don't have the advert just going to your home page.

- **Continuously monitor and refine** – The biggest mistake business owners make is jumping in blind and not reviewing their data to find ways to improve the performance of the campaign. In order to be successful with PPC, you need to analyse and adjust constantly.

- **Ensure your website is mobile friendly** – As discussed earlier in this chapter, it is imperative that your website is mobile friendly.

Search engine optimisation (SEO)

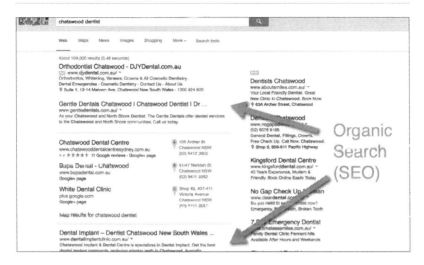

Search engine optimisation (SEO) is the on-going process of making sure your website performs as well as possible on specific search engine searches. The key distinction between paid and organic search marketing is that with search engine optimisation, you get the visitors you earn. Whereas with pay per click, you get the visitors you pay for.

Why optimise your website?

Success is based on being top of search rankings. The top-ranked website for a search does better than the second. The top few get many times more visits than the results at the bottom of the first page, which in turn get many times more clicks than results on page two, etc.

You should be optimising your website to get high rankings. Aim to get in the top five or ten results for your chosen search terms or keywords.

How to improve your search ranking

With SEO, you attract visitors by developing a high-quality website. Improving your SEO takes time and work. Expect to spend six months on SEO work before you see a significant improvement.

At first glance, this may seem like a disadvantage. But it's actually a good thing. SEO forces you to do things you should be doing anyway (things like content development, website usability improvement, and online networking). Your website will come out of it better than when you started.

> I really wish that, once and for all, I could deliver the message that there is no simple way to get on the first page of Google. If you get approached by an SEO or website company that guarantees getting on page one of Google instantly, ignore them immediately. Please delete their email or put down the phone.

SEO made simple

Finding out how to get on the first page of Google may feel like a complex and overwhelming task. Following some simple steps makes it possible to create a website that does well in Google ranking search results.

Get an expert to build your website

The best thing that you can do to increase your rankings with Google is to run a quality website. Hire a professional and do this properly.

Use keywords

When someone uses a search engine, they type in one or more words describing what they are looking for, e.g. 'Dentist Sydney or 'Invisalign'. These words or phrases are known as keywords. You need good keywords within your website. Therefore, when patients search for relevant keywords, your website appears as early as possible in the list of results.

The keywords you use in your website need to relate to your content and words that users are actually looking for. Use Google Analytics to find the best keywords for your business. Research keywords so that you don't waste effort writing about things people don't care about. Then, use those keywords in your website text, while being careful not to overload the text with the keywords.

Create quality original content

It is critical to focus on the quality of the text in your website. This text needs to be unique. If you are tempted to steal text from other people's websites, don't, you will be penalised by Google. Also, if your website company 'provides' text, ensure that this is written for you and is not the same as the text they provide the rest of their clients. Again, you will be penalised for duplicate text.

Some content tips:

- Each page should have over three hundred words of text.

- Focus on creating a large number of unique pages.

- You must ensure that different content is on each page.

- Ensure correct grammar and spelling.

- Don't separate your brand from your content. Write about the services you are offering.

- Post unique and interesting content on a regular basis that you know people will want to share.

- Add all your content onto your main website (i.e. don't have a separate blog website).

- Do not duplicate your content over different pages of your website or steal someone else's content. Focus on creating quality content that's all your own.

- Create a separate page on your website for each service that you offer.

Ensure your website is usable on multiple devices and screen resolutions

If your website fails to meet common user expectations (readable text, easy navigation, no horizontal scrolling, etc.) on desktops, laptops, tablets, and smartphones, you will be penalised by Google. Talk to your website designer about making the necessary adjustments to your website to ensure that it is mobile friendly and works on all devises.

On-page SEO

You need good on-page SEO. You or your website developer need to ensure that certain settings are configured and set correctly on every page of your website (Title, Description, and Header tags).

Create separate pages for each keyword or key word phrase, i.e. don't have a general services page, have separate pages that focus on each service (e.g. a page for crowns, a page for Invisalign, etc.).

These pages then need to have the on-page SEO settings correctly configured.

Incorporate appropriate images

Google looks for good quality images and pictures. Buy or create images that match your text and add to the overall website experience.

Don't steal images from other websites as it is a breach of copyright, it will effect your SEO and you could end up with a fine. Buy images from reputable stock image websites or, even better, have your own taken.

Create quality back-links

Back-links are when another website, preferably one that gets more hits than yours, links to your page. Google will know your website is legitimate from users sharing your content around the web. More back-links mean better search rankings.

Remember, you want these back-links to be quality. Google can tell the difference. Do not spam comment sections trying to build back-links for yourself. You will be penalised for this behaviour.

Speak to your website company or marketing consultant to find out the best way to build quality back-links to your website.

Use social media

Social media likes and shares are rewarded more than ever these days with Google, especially with subjects that are currently relevant. This means that you should create social media accounts and try to build a base of followers who will like your pages and share them with friends.

(See social media section below.)

Update your website regularly

Google rewards sites that have regular maintenance and updates. This means if you've been ignoring your website, you're in trouble. Find small ways to update it with new blog posts every couple of weeks, photos from events, case studies, etc.

(See blog section below.)

Monitor and revise

Google uses many tools and algorithms that are updated regularly to determine the order that websites are displayed in search results. On a monthly basis, you need to monitor your Google Analytics and Google Console (previously called Google Webmaster) reports and make any changes required. Remember to get in the experts to help you further.

The importance of citations

A citation is where other websites and online directories (e.g. Yellow Pages, True Local, Google) mention your practice's name, address, website, and phone number.

For local SEO and earning a higher placement in Google's local search listings, citations are very important. Having your practice listed on other websites helps to make your website appear more credible and legitimate from the perspective of search engines.

Have your business listed on third party websites

You need to ensure that your practice is listed with all of the large directories. Have your business name, address, and phone number listed on trustworthy and authoritative websites.

Ensure that your details are identical

It is also critical that your practice details are identical. Your name, address, and phone number should be listed exactly the same way in each listing.

For example, you might sometimes write your address in two ways: '2/414 The High Street' and 'Suite 2, 414 The High Street'. All of your directory listings need to be written in exactly the same way.

Citations are important and should be kept top of mind. Make sure that yours are up to date and written in an identical way.

Which search engine marketing strategy is best for me?

Practices often reach a point where they feel they must choose between search engine optimisation and pay per click. I am often asked:

- Which one is better suited for the business model?

- Which one is more effective in driving traffic, leads, and sales?

- Should they be used simultaneously or in isolation?

When to use pay per click

For fast results, PPC marketing (such as Google Adwords) can help you drive targeted visitors to your website in a hurry. It is also good if you have a smaller budget.

But it has a significant downside. With pay per click, you have to pay for every click to your website. And the moment you cancel the campaign, the traffic stream stops.

When to use search engine optimisation

SEO has more long-term advantages than PPC. All practices need to have an SEO strategy in place. To improve your organic search engine rankings, you need to develop keyword-rich content and a strong linking profile. It may take a while (over six months) to accomplish these things, but the results outlast the efforts.

So in the long run, SEO is better value than PPC.

When to combine pay per click with search engine optimisation

If you have the budget, and to make your online advertising more effective, it is a good idea to combine pay per click advertising with search engine optimisation. When PPC and SEO are combined, it can result in a practice dominating the top of Google search results, both in the organic results as well as the paid ads.

When a patient sees that a brand has a presence in both areas, they are more likely to click through, as they see that practice as influential and a leader. This also allows you to cover all areas, as some consumers prefer to trust organic results more (knowing that the position wasn't purchased) and some tend to click on the paid search results more. Cover as much of the Google search results real estate as possible.

Warning

I feel that I need to warn you about the many unethical companies that are out there in the online world. I guarantee that you will be bombarded with emails and calls from companies saying that they can help you with your search engine marketing and pay per click campaigns.

I hear horror stories on a daily basis from practices that have been paying small fortunes to get these services and have been taken for a ride in terrible ways. There are many companies out there that will try and take your money in this area.

My advice is for you to do your research and ask around. Find out whom other businesses use and whom they recommend. Do not go for the cheapest company as you will invariably get what you pay for; pick a company that is local (i.e. not overseas) and that you can speak to and interact with.

If your gut feeling is that you are not getting what you paid for, please act on it. Do some research and get a second opinion.

Google My Business

Google My Business has become critical in helping potential patients find the business they are looking for. With most of your potential patients turning to a friend or the Internet to find a dentist, you should have a presence on Google My Business to increase your opportunity of being found by someone new.

How to update your Google My Business listing

Google My Business listings will show local listings in almost every city and these listings will appear on the first page of the Google results. Many patients will search these listings before using any other search engine.

You need to be placed in one of the top positions. Here are the factors that affect your Google My Business ranking in the search engine results:

1. The content, keywords, pictures, and videos on your Google My Business page.

2. Your reviews on Google.

3. Citations (business listings with your address) on other sites and directories throughout the Internet.

4. Your proximity to the searcher.

5. Your main website SEO.

It is much easier to plan your online marketing strategy when you know which factors will improve your ranking. Most local business owners are not using this free online resource to its full potential and as a result are losing out on business opportunities.

These are some effective ways of using this free online tool to expand your business and jump ahead of your local competitors. Get on Google My Business and get ahead of your competition.

Setting up your Google My Business listing

1. **Claim your listing** – Go to: http://www.google.com.au/business/

2. **Verify your listing** – Once you have claimed your free listing, Google will contact your business by phone or mail to verify your details to ensure that you are a legitimate business.

3. **Optimise your listing** – Complete as much of the information as possible. The aim is to provide your visitor with

a complete profile and description of your business. Include contact details (ensuring that details are associated with the town/city you are targeting if you have more than one office), opening hours, at least a three-hundred-word summary of your business (using crucial keywords and services), categories, and try to upload at least five photos plus one video.

Google My Business steps

Remove duplicate pages

If the name, address, or phone number of your business is listed more than once on Google My Business, delete all duplicate listings. You can do this with your login details or by contacting Google directly.

Choose appropriate categories on your page

Choose categories that accurately describe your business (i.e. dentist, cosmetic dentist, dental clinic, etc.).

Be consistent with your business name, address, and phone number

Ensure that your business name, address, and phone number on the page are identical to those shown on your website.

Add a Google map of your business location to your website

To do this, search for your address on Google Maps, then click the 'Link' button to get the embed code for the map. Include this code on your website.

The importance of a blog

In today's online world, I now recommend that all of my dental clients seriously think about blogging.

When it comes to blogging, the more you commit to it, the greater the reward will be:

- 57% of marketers who blog monthly have acquired a patient through their blog.

- This number jumps up to 82% when they blog every day.

- 43% of people surveyed have acquired a patient through their blog this year alone.

- Over 60% of companies now publish a blog.[13]

What exactly is blogging?

A blog is the part of your website where you can add dynamic and ever-changing content. Blogging is the act of creating content to a blog.

It is important to note that when you are blogging for your business, your blog posts are about a particular subject matter related to your practice.

Why does my practice need a blog?

A blog can become one of the most valuable tools in your online marketing toolbox, if you do it correctly.

If a website is the hub of your online presence, a blog located on your website is its heart. A blog allows you to tell stories about your practice and provide important information, showing your patients (and potential patients) that you know what you're talking about. A blog provides much of the search engine optimisation needed to get better placement in search engine results.

Thoughtful blogging strengthens patient relationships.

The benefits of blogging

The benefits of blogging for dentists include the following:

- Shows patients and prospective patients that you care.

- Makes you more approachable to patients.

- Attracts new patients and increases treatment plan acceptance.

- Educates patients about the services that you provide.

- Increases career satisfaction for your team.

- Reinforces to your team that what you provide is important.

What should you blog about?

Make your blog content interesting, engaging, thoughtful, relevant, and useful. It should have great value to your readers. Do not write content specifically for search engines at the expense of your audience and do not focus on the clinical aspects of dentistry, which may be boring to many people. Talk about dentistry (and non-dental topics) in very human ways.

Blog about topics that people care about. Here are some examples:

- **Offers and promos** – Blog about your latest offers or the services that you are trying to promote.

- **News** – Talk about news such as changes to your practice and your staff; any updates taking place in your dental office.

- **Information and education articles** – Talk about oral-health and how it affects overall health.

- **Real stories and case studies** – People love real stories. Whether you use your own little anecdotes or patient case studies, real stories are great.

- **Children** – Appeal to readers who are parents. Explain dental topics relevant to children, tweens, and teens.

- **Quiz** – Blogs can also be in quiz format. Use quizzes to learn about your patients.

- **Top Ten** – Everyone wants a quick, worthwhile read, e.g. Top Ten Whitening Systems, Top Ten Reasons People Choose Veneers, etc.

- **A Secret** – Give readers an inside scoop, e.g. The Secret to Lifelong Teeth Whitening, The Secret to Fresh Breath, The Secret to Keeping Teeth for Life, etc.

- **Hot Topics** – Most people want to look beautiful. Turn Hollywood news into fodder for your blog.

Blogging tips

- Try and blog at least once a month.

- Make your blog content rich with a minimum of three hundred words per post.

- Think about answering patients' frequently asked questions.

- Always include an image.

Images for your blogs

Always include images in your blog posts. Successful blog posts that receive the most social shares usually also have a common characteristic. These blogs include some well-placed pictures to break up content and emphasise certain points.

Caution – Do not steal images from other websites; either use your own or purchase them from reputable stock image websites (see Resources).

Repurposing your blog content

Creating new content for your online presence can be challenging. Repurposing your blog content can help with this.

One key benefit of repurposing content (aka finding new ways to recycle or up-cycle your existing content) is the time it can save you in the content creation process. Repurposing your content breathes new life into valuable information. It takes what was old and makes it new again, offering it up to a whole new audience in an updated format. Not only is it budget friendly, it also saves time while prolonging the shelf life of your online assets.

Repurposing content has a number of benefits, such as:

- Getting an SEO boost. Multiple pieces of content around the same topic can generate additional opportunities to target a desired keyword.

- Reaching a new audience. In many cases, your original piece of content may have only made an impact with one group of customers.

- Repetition can be an essential part of reinforcing a message. Marketing's Rule of Seven states that people need to hear your message seven times before they make a decision. Repurposing goes a long ways towards reaching this quota.

- Gaining extra authority. Publishing quality content in a variety of places on a single topic can help raise your profile in the industry and teach others to regard you as an expert.

Below are some different ways to repurpose old content. If there's one commonality in all these, it's this: Add value to the original. Content repurposing doesn't just mean that you reuse an old piece of content again and again. You need to alter it to make it fresh and appealing to a new audience.

1. **Create new blog posts and articles** – High-quality content can spinoff more high-quality content, and the audience can benefit from both.

2. **Create a presentation** – Interesting statistics, meaningful quotes, and actionable advice can make for effective slides, and the resulting presentation can offer an easy-to-read recap of your original content.

3. **Build an infographic** – An infographic is a complete summary of the content of your blog in a visual outline. If you have a lot of data in your article, infographics are a great way to relate data or merely to break up an article into just the major talking points.

4. **Create a Pinterest instructographic** – This is like a mini infographic, but focused more on the how-to aspect.

5. **Refresh and republish old posts** – Modify old content so that it has more up-to-date information and statistics, then republish it as a new blog post.

6. **Repost and re-promote to social media** – You can share your previous blog on different social media channels, in different time zones, reaching new followers, and testing variations of headlines.

7. **Create an eBook** – Expanding your existing content into an eBook seems like a logical step in the content process. It's amazing how many high-quality eBooks began as blog posts.

8. **Convert to a podcast or video** – Chances are that some of your audience prefers content they don't have to read. In this sense, podcasts and videos could be one of the most important

repurposing methods because they open up a whole new way to connect with others.

Engaging in social media

Why you should consider using social media

There is a lot of talk about social media marketing for business. Some dental practices are jumping on the social media bandwagon. Other dental practices have an intuitive hunch that there is something to all of this, but they're just not yet sure what it is.

I get asked all the time, 'Do I really need social media for my dental practice?'

The staggering statistics speak for themselves. In December 2015, Facebook had fourteen million Australian users and YouTube had just less then fourteen million users.[14] A recent survey in the USA found that 92% of orthodontists used Facebook, followed by 72% of general dentists, and 70% of paediatric dentists.[15]

What can you use social media for?

You can use social media to:

- **Create a credible image** – Show that there are real people behind the dentistry and that you are on top of all the latest techniques and research.

- **Boost your website traffic** – Include links in posts to your website. If people are interested in your services, they will click through to discover more about your practice.

- **Improve your SEO rankings** – SEO is influenced by 'social signals'. These are Likes, Tweets, +1's, Pins, Shares, etc., that individuals attribute to a webpage. When a specific page, whether a blog post or YouTube video, has a wealth of 'social signals', its SEO-value increases.

- **Have fun** – Get creative with your social media account and make dentistry more familiar and approachable to patients.

- **Keep up with your competitors** – This is the future of marketing. Get on top of social media to attract the potential patients searching online before your competitors do.

Forward-thinking practices are beginning to understand the significance of being visible on social media.

Social media strategies

With social media, dentists can easily share their knowledge and present themselves as real people, not just a name and a logo. Regardless of where your practice is in its social media marketing evolution, whether just starting out or already an expert, here are some strategies that may help:

Attract new patients through visibility

Marketing has changed. Today, it's is about engaging with communities and delivering services with stories that spread. Increasing top-of-mind awareness with existing patients leads to more referrals.

Word-of-mouth advertising has been around forever but today the widespread use, ease, and scalability of social media tools mean that word-of-mouth has moved online.

Studies have shown that a very low percentage of your existing patients actually know (or think about) the scope of services that you offer. Publishing content and educating current patients about a wide variety of related topics through your blog and social media directly leads to increased knowledge, awareness, referral potential, and greater case acceptance.

Increase patient loyalty through culture

In the old days, most practices believed that their brand primarily centred on a logo and static website. Not any more. Successful brands are about online connections, likeable transparency, and dynamic content.

Through social media, patients will pick up on a very powerful message. That you listen, care, are open and honest, and that you treat people, not teeth. The perception is that you are leading edge in everything you do, including your dental services.

Promotions, offers, contests, check-ins, and deals create interest and viral buzz, people enjoy sharing them. Contests and giveaways can range from the extremely simple and inexpensive to more the complex and costly. Either way, when compared to traditional marketing (magazine ads, direct mail, email newsletters, etc.), these types of promotions provide great value and traction.

Attain practice growth and a mindset change

Social media storytelling reinforces through text and visuals (photos and video), that what you are doing matters. While I don't mean to oversell this benefit, I have seen these outward manifestations of in-practice cultures not only strengthen patient relationships and increase business, but also positively impact team dynamics as well.

The dental practices that most successfully use social media marketing are the ones committed to business on a deeply personal level. These are the practices that consider revenue increases both in terms of traditional, short-term ROI and as a natural, long-term outgrowth of better serving people.

Prioritising your social media activities

The most common question I'm asked is, 'Which social media network is the most important to focus on?'

Each social media network has its various advantages and disadvantages. The main thing is to be present where your target market is. You need to decide where is most appropriate for your practice, and where you can effectively execute your social media marketing strategy.

Priority 1: Facebook

Facebook acts as an excellent supplement to your practice's website, encouraging constant interaction with patients. It's where you can tell the story of your company, intrigue your viewers, and reach the millions online.

Ask your patients:

- To 'check-in' on Facebook when they come to your office (they do this on their smartphones).

- To 'Like' your practice page.

- To post a picture, video, or comment if they want to, perhaps about their visit to your practice.

Your posts should be personal and frequent (ideally daily), but not clinical. And you should always comment on any post a patient makes.

SEO Tip: Include your keyword targets in the profile page's URL and in the description. Use relevant hashtags in posts (e.g. #dentist). Link posts back to your website. Include a link to your Facebook page from your website.

Priority 2: Google+

As stated before, Google+ is important because Google is able to enhance its search engine results with information gathered from users' social circles. At the time of writing spending time on Google+ should be a priority for your practice.

Priority 3: YouTube

YouTube is searched extensively. Many people would much rather watch a video than read something. Every video that you make should show up on YouTube, Facebook, Google+, and your website. It is important to note that YouTube is also owned by Google. The more often you post a video, the better it will be for your practice.

(Read more on YouTube and the use of videos to promote your practice below.)

Priority 4: Instagram

Instagram has seen 32% growth in Australia over the past twelve months, now serving five million monthly Australian users.[16]

Instagram is widely used and is owned by Facebook. You can take interesting photos of your patients, particularly before-and-after shots, or provide behind-the-scenes footage for your followers, giving them a taste of your practice, team, values, and services. Share relevant and useful information in the caption, like location details, team names, and services. Offer followers exclusive benefits and make your business more personable.

Priority 5: Twitter

Twitter is a great social media tool for enhancing your public relations (PR) and building your 'brand'. You can enhance your 'know', 'like', and 'trust' factor through simply tweeting regularly and sharing with your followers. Share day-to-day happenings or tweet relevant links and news.

It is easy to be active on Twitter because what you post is so short. It can be very effective in your practice for alerting patients of openings in your schedule. You can post pictures, videos, and alert your Twitter audience every time you post a blog on your website.

SEO Tip: Take the time to reach out, follow, and re-tweet posts of like-minded influencers and businesses. The greater the following you can cultivate, the greater exposure (and social signal potential) your tweets will have.

Priority 6: LinkedIn

LinkedIn has the highest business-focus of all social media networks. It serves as an excellent tool to create exposure among an educated and professional audience.

You should not so much expect to get many patients from here, but it is great to improve your credibility. Use LinkedIn to reconnect with old colleagues, recruit associates and staff, and join professional groups. Being a LinkedIn member enhances credibility and visibility, as well as having SEO value.

SEO Tip: Connect with as many colleagues, patients, and friends as you can. A strong LinkedIn following will increase your page's search engine authority, in addition to increasing the likelihood that your LinkedIn posts get shared.

Priority 7: Pinterest, Periscope, etc.

Whilst there are other social media networks, they will be of lower value when trying to attract patients. You may find some practices taking advantage of one or two of them, particularly Pinterest, which has a very high amount of user activity, but for the most part your energy should be spent elsewhere.

SEO Tip: When building your Pinterest page, use keywords to describe your pinboards, as well as to define the URL and description of your profile page (e.g. Sydney dentist, cosmetic dentistry Sydney, etc.)

Social media tips

The most successful and 'liked' activities on social media have some common threads. Use these as guidelines for your activity:

- **Be fun** – Successful practices make social media fun for team members and patients. It's not a chore.

- **Do the unexpected** – Throw out the boring and be a little adventuresome.

- **Be involved in the community** – Nearly every thriving practice does some good in their community. And they talk about it online.

- **Use patient images** – Many patients are happy to help you in your efforts. Remember to ask permission.

- **Share team members' personalities** – Patients and prospective patients become loyal to people they know and like.

- **Link back to your website** – When posting tips or news remember to include a link back to a relevant page on your website. This will improve your Google ranking.

- **Mix your posts** – Have a great mix of educational, fun, and promotional posts on social media. Too much of one will be overpowering. Try and have a balance.

- **Experiment** – Use a small part of your marketing budget to boost certain posts and promotions. Test and see what works best for your practice and patients

- **Be yourself** – Be genuine and don't try to be anything that you and your team aren't.

Social media summary

The important rule to remember when starting with social media is to build up gradually. Start using only as many platforms as you can handle well. Be regular, be friendly, be fun, and be as non-commercial as you can.

- Step one is to create accounts.

- Make social media part of someone's job in the practice.

- Spend fifteen to thirty minutes a day composing posts.

- Be consistent and keep it fresh.

- Get releases from your patients for all photos and video.

- Be familiar with the latest social media guidelines from ARPRA.

Videos and YouTube

With over one billion users, and with the number of hours people are watching YouTube each month up 50% year on year, YouTube can be a powerful platform for marketing a business online.[17]

To do it well, go beyond simply posting random videos of your practice or sharing your thoughts. Here are some statistics:[18]

- The average Internet user spends 88% more time on a website with video.[19]

- 64% of consumers are more likely to buy a service or a product after watching a video about it.[20]

- 70% of marketing professionals report that video converts better than any other medium.[21]

- Visitors who view videos stay on websites an average of two minutes longer than those who don't view videos.[22]

The advantages of video

There are millions of websites on the Internet and millions more being launched. Videos on a website are a valuable asset as they show people the dentists behind the practice, letting them connect with the human side of the business. Potential patients will be more comfortable calling your office.

Online videos increase credibility and authority. When visitors to your website can see that you are knowledgeable about your specific services and issues with dental care, they will view you as the authority and one that they can trust.

With YouTube being the second largest search engine in the world, uploading your videos onto your website and YouTube and then optimising them to ensure high rankings will drive more traffic to your website.

What type of video?

I am often asked what type of videos I would recommend a practice to have, professional or self-produced videos.

I recommend that you consider both. A professionally produced video to show an office tour and practice introduction will help to present a professional practice. Meanwhile, self-made videos could be made for practice updates and staff or specialist interviews.

Video ideas

Here are some video ideas:

- **Slideshows** – A slideshow is a series of images/photographs that are displayed in order. Consider showing your entire practice and/or pictures of your patients (with their permission).

- **Interviews** – Consider interviewing your patients about their dental issues, explaining in the video how you would help to address those issues.

- **Recent events** – During your clinic's anniversary or open day, video the occasion and then upload onto your website/YouTube for online users to see.

- **Tutorials** – Provide step-by-step instructions on various dental processes, practices or treatment descriptions such as Invisalign and IV sedation.

- **Reviews** – Explain a new product or technology and how it works. Patients and fellow dentists will want to know more.

- **Vlog** – A vlog is a blog created from video blog posts. Simply make a short video of yourself in your clinic and talk about your day, giving your viewers a tour of your practice.

- **Music** – Do you or a member of your team like to sing or dance? Some of the best practice videos that I have seen show dental teams singing, dancing, or even playing instruments. This shows your viewers and future patients that your practice also knows how to have fun.

Video key points

A few key points to remember:

- Get signed permission from everyone you shoot, including your team members.

- Watch other videos to see what you like and how they are created.

- Keep your videos short. 59% of viewers will watch a video to completion that is less than one minute.[23]

The marketing videos you create should include the following elements:

- A keyword-researched headline.

- A clear editorial message (do not try to accomplish too much in one video).

- A call to action (tell the viewer to do something, such as subscribing to your channel).

Group deal websites

Over the last few years, there has been an explosion of group deal websites or coupon websites.

Group deal websites offer products and services at significantly reduced prices on the condition that a minimum number of buyers make the purchase. In recent times, group-buying websites have emerged as a major player in the online shopping industry.

Typically, these websites feature a 'deal of the day', with the deal starting once a set number of people agree to buy the product or service.

Examples of websites that are popular in Australia are:

- Living Social
- Groupon
- Cudo
- Scoopon
- Catch Of The Day
- Dental Deal Online

I have seen many dentists using these websites to promote group discounts such as teeth whitening, Invisalign, implants, veneers, and dental examinations. They can be used to attract a large number of people into your practice.

However, I would recommend that you think about these services before using them. They tend to attract the people that like to shop around for a bargain and are much less likely to attract the type of long-term patients that you need for your practice. Once again, this comes back to knowing your ideal patient.

If you do want to try this strategy, I recommend that you:

- Think about the number of services you will offer.
- Are prepared for the huge amount of calls from people wanting to book in for the offer.
- Recognise that many of the people will come just the once for the offer and you need to gather their details and market to this group to try to convert them to long-term patients paying your regular (not discounted) fees.

Attracting patients in print

Print advertising

Print advertising used to be at the centre of all advertising because you had little other choice. It can be effective, but it is expensive and hit and miss. It is incredibly hard to track the ROI of your advert.

With the onset of digital marketing, print advertising is becoming less popular. It's often not the most cost-effective solution for advertising your dental practice, as it tends to be disproportionately expensive.

However, there are still opportunities to attract new patients with print advertising. You just need to compare a potential campaign to online advertising in terms of reach and frequency.

Before considering placing a print advert, you need to really look at the demographic information of the publication. Is this a great fit for your ideal patient and target market? Think about the readers' ages, average household income, location, etc.

Look at your budget and see what frequency you can afford with the publication. If you cannot afford to run the advert frequently then don't do it. Remember, frequency is more powerful than reach. You need to run a campaign with a series of ads over a period of time to build brand awareness.

Your print advert

If you do decide to go ahead with print advertising, you need to make sure that your advert grabs your target's attention. Don't just put your name and practice address there, you'll be wasting your time.

Your advert needs to be relevant to your ideal patient and needs to hold their attention. Each advert should focus on what your ideal patient cares about, not what you as a dentist care about. Think back to their needs, fears, and wants.

It is essential that your advert should motivate them to do something. It should give them a reason to contact you through a strong call to action. Making an offer is often a great reason to take action (such as to call, or go to your website, etc.).

I speak to many dentists that have been running the same print advert for years without ever changing it or reviewing it. As with all types of marketing, best practice is to test several adverts and track their response. If one advert has the best response then run that advert until you have more to test. If several get a similar response, I recommended that you alternate between them.

Practice brochure

I recommend that all dental practices have a well-written, professionally-designed brochure that establishes the identity or brand of the practice. Differentiation can be achieved by stressing education and training and by relating experiences with specific patient groups, such as seniors.

Information should be patient-focused, e.g. stressing the benefits and outcomes of your services.

A brochure should also include professional photos of the dentists and team. Be sure the overall design look complements your logo and signage to convey a unified image.

Flyers

This is an old way of communication but still very effective. Flyers are cheap to print and easy to distribute locally. They are a great way to promote a new practice or to boost patient numbers for a new associate.

You can distribute your flyers to local residents via a letterbox drop or handing them out at a train station or shopping centre. Make sure they are designed well, are eye-catching, and, most importantly, include a strong call to action.

A common mistake I see is flyers only talking about the practice and saying something like 'accepting new patients'. To maximise the results, include a special offer, e.g. a reduced or free check-up and clean, or a teeth-whitening offer. Put an expiry date on these offers and make it clear how they patients can claim these.

Yellow Pages print directory

Taking out classifieds adverts in the Yellow Pages directory was once a mainstay. But these times have passed. Ask yourself, your staff, patients, and friends when the last time was they looked for any new service in the Yellow Pages diretory.

My recommendation would be to spend little or nothing on Yellow Pages print advertising unless you live in a small rural area with few competitors. Yellow Pages print adverts are not targeted and, in most cases, they are still bursting with dozens of adverts, which makes it impossible to stand out.

Direct mail

Targeted properly, a direct mail campaign can get the phone ringing. Mailing your practice brochure or flyers is a great way to gain introduction in target households, and the piece might be kept for future reference. Timing also can influence the effectiveness of direct mail. Stay away from the summer, when many families are away on vacation, and receive the high volumes of direct mail. September is a excellent month for direct-mail marketing of cosmetic dentistry because the start of spring gets people thinking more about their appearance at the same time that tax refund checks start hitting the mailboxes.

Promotional items

As a rule, avoid investing too much in pens, coffee cups, and other items that display your name but do little to differentiate you from your competition.

It's nice to hand patients a promotional gift, but don't depend on such trinkets for lasting benefits. Consider using them only to reward patients for performing an action such as 'liking' your social media page or filling in a patient survey.

Broadcast advertising

One of the common mistakes people make when buying broadcast advertising, i.e. TV or radio advertising, is forgetting the reach of their practice. For a rural practice, your reach will be around

50km or more, for a suburban dentist 15km. If you are located in the middle of Sydney or Melbourne, it could be as small as a few kilometres or even just a number of streets.

With broadcast advertising, the more the reach, the more you pay. If you are a general dentist, working in a city suburb with no specialisation, do you really want to pay to advertise to 40,000 people across the metro area where very few will be in your target radius?

It can also be incredibly expensive. The closer you are to a major metropolitan area, the higher the price.

Considering your demographic

Think about whom you are trying to reach. Spend time researching the demographics of the TV or radio station, including average household income, household spending, age, and gender. Do not take the sales person's word for it. You really do need to check for yourself.

I meet many practices that have been sold to by TV and radio stations. Their sales people are paid to appeal to your ego and to sell you on 'getting your brand out there'. Please do not get sold on this. They are paid to sell adverts and are not interested in the success of your business.

However, having said that, there are some cases where this kind of advertising could work for you:

- **If you have a speciality** – Radio marketing in the dental community is best used when advertising specialty dental procedures. Something that patients can't find at every dentist and are willing to travel to get. If you have a specialisation that provides your dental practice with a significant competitive advantage (for example ozone or holistic dentistry), broadcast marketing advertising might be an excellent way to spread your message.

- **If you are in a small town or rural area** – The price of advertising will be significantly cheaper in these areas and could well be worth looking into. Rural dentists often find that radio and TV allow them to reach patients in a large geographical area. Also, rural patients are far more likely than those in a city to travel long distances for dental care.

- **If you are a dental chain or have a large number of practices in one area** – If you have a number of practices spread throughout the area that the broadcast media reaches, you have more chance of success with this kind of advertising.

If you do decide to try broadcast advertising then invest in a good advert that is well shot/recorded and has been scripted by a professional organisation. Include clear and effective messaging. You need to explain what makes your practice different and talk about the benefits – not a long list of services.

Broadcast advertising needs to tick all three of the following boxes so you don't waste your money:

1. Meets the demographic of your ideal patient and target market.

2. Is at a price that means you can afford frequency.

3. Has the correct reach for your practice.

'Fish where the fish are'

I was once given a most memorable piece of marketing advice, which has stuck with me to this day: 'If you want to catch a fish, you need to fish where the fish are.'

This is a way of testing the suitability of any particular type of marketing. It starts with identifying your ideal patient, their behaviour patterns, and what media types they use. You can then test the suitably of any particular advertising against this knowledge.

For example, if your ideal patient is a young, child-free executive who wants cosmetic dentistry, then advertising in the Yellow Pages is a waste of money.

Depending on your practice, you'll have a preference for where to focus your efforts, but most businesses will embrace both an online and print presence, albeit to different extents.

In summary

There are so many options to attract new patients, so many 'shiny new object' social media platforms to play with. The greatest piece of advice when trying to attract new patients is to get your basics right. Before going out and spending significant time, money, and effort on any type of advertising or online marketing – make sure you have the basics right.

In this day and age, this means your website needs to be the best you can afford. It needs to look and feel like your physical practice. It needs to be in line with your values and needs to be an online expression of you and your team.

No matter what else you do and how much money you spend on other forms of marketing, people are always going to look at your website. It will be the first place they visit. Make sure that this is up to scratch or you will be wasting your time and effort on all other forms of marketing.

Step 4 – Checklist

	YES	NO
Have you addressed the reach versus frequency of your marketing?	○	○
Have you written your external marketing message?	○	○
Have you reviewed your website?	○	○
Do you offer online booking?	○	○
Have you claimed your Google+ listing?	○	○
Have you checked your online citations?	○	○
Do you understand the terms used within search engine marketing (SEO, PPC, SEM, organic search)?	○	○
Have you assessed your website's SEO performance?	○	○
Are you using pay per click advertising?	○	○
Have you assessed your PPC performance?	○	○

Are you blogging regularly?   ◯   ◯

Are you engaging in social media?   ◯   ◯

Do you have online videos?   ◯   ◯

Are you attracting patients with print?   ◯   ◯

Have you assessed your print advertising?   ◯   ◯

Do you have an up-to-date and effective practice   ◯   ◯
brochure?

Do you use promotional items?   ◯   ◯

Have you assessed if TV/radio advertising is right   ◯   ◯
for your practice?

Bonus Material

To download checklists and documents
that accompany this book:

Go to www.fullybookeddentist.com/resources

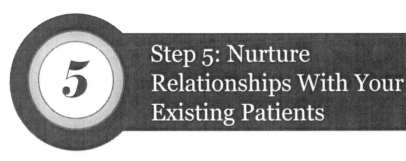

The value of patient retention

A satisfied customer is the best business strategy of all.

Michael LeBoeuf

Many practices make the mistake of focusing only on gaining new patients. They fail to effectively address the need to retain those they already have.

Did you know that the most valuable asset that a practice has is its existing patient base? Every practice wants and needs new patients, but your surest and most predictable source of new revenue is right under your nose. It comes from the loyal patients who already know your practice.

It's also far easier (about 50% easier according to Marketing Metrics) to sell to existing patients than to new prospects. Acquiring new patients is expensive (five to ten times the cost of retaining an existing one), but the average spend of a repeat patient is a whopping 67% more.

There are further staggering statistics on the value of existing patient reactivation versus new patient acquisition:

- The probability of selling to an existing patient is 60 to 70%, while the probability of selling to a new prospect is 5 to 20%.[24]

- A 2% increase in patient retention has the same effect as decreasing costs by 10%.[25]

- Attracting new patients will cost your company five times more than keeping an existing patient.[26]

- A 5% reduction in the patient defection rate can increase profits by 5 to 95%.[27]

Why do patients leave?

The average dental practice loses between 15 to 20% of their patient base per annum.[28] Yet only 7 to 8% will move out of your area each year.

Therefore, the rest of your patients are leaving for other reasons. If you are not tracking your numbers, this steady erosion of your patients can go unnoticed for years. When you do notice, it may well be too late.

It is critical to start monitoring, stop this steady loss of business, and turn your existing patients into loyal ones.

One main reason for patients leaving a practice is that the practice does not stay in touch. If you don't stay in touch with your patients, they will think that you don't care, they won't know what other services you are offering that may be of interest to them and their network of family and friends, and they wont be educated in understanding why they need to come in for regular check-ups or to complete their treatment plan.

Regular communication with your existing patients is critical. Internal marketing is the name given to this communication.

Internal marketing

Internal dental marketing is all about building strong, lasting relationships with your patients. As we have seen, it is far less expensive to do what is necessary to retain an existing patient than it is to attract a new dental patient through external marketing.

Practices should use internal marketing with their focus on keeping the patients they already have coming back. There are some key things you can do from an internal marketing standpoint to help you reduce your marketing costs and drive referrals from existing patients.

Developing internal marketing strategies

There are so many easy and inexpensive or even cost-free things you and your staff can do to enhance the patient experience. Just start with the little things and you will begin to build a culture in your dental practice that will make your patients feel good about you and more likely to stay.

Remember that your current patients are the audience for your internal marketing message. With internal marketing, you're talking to people who already know you, so it feels more comfortable.

Listed below are some best practice items that should be included within your internal dental marketing activity:

- Greeting dental patients with a smile.
- Answering your phone in person on the first or second ring.
- Calling a patient at home after a difficult or long session to see how he or she is feeling.
- Sending birthday cards to patients.
- Publishing a patient newsletter – printed and digital.
- Putting up reception area signage.
- Printing a referral brochure.
- Undertaking patient satisfaction surveys.
- Sending patient 'thank you's.
- Implementing a rewards program for loyal patients.
- Establishing on-hold marketing.
- Sending birthday cards.
- Educating patients.
- Holding events.
- Promoting your website.
- Undertaking email marketing.
- Posting on social media.
- Running offers, promotions, and competitions.
- Sending appointment reminders.
- Keeping in touch via text messaging.
- Maximising recalls.

Sending email newsletters

I believe that email communication is one of the most cost-effective marketing methods you can implement. Start collecting email addresses as early as you can. Even if you don't currently have an email strategy prepared, these will prove very useful at a future time.

Email marketing campaigns give you the opportunity to distribute information to a wide audience of patients at a relatively competitive rate. Research shows that email marketing has one of the best return on investment ratios.[29]

A growing number of professionals use newsletter marketing to build their practices. Newsletters are ideally suited and highly effective for the unique marketing needs of professional practices. Unlike traditional advertising, newsletters are not viewed as self-serving, because each issue provides valuable information.

Email newsletters benefits

The benefits of email newsletters include the following:

- They enhance your practice's reputation.
- They increase the lifetime value of your patients.
- They leverage your other marketing efforts.
- They provide instantaneous, easily-tracked results.
- There is an opportunity for your patients to easily and immediately interact with you.
- You can promote dialogue with them.

- They provide a higher response rate because they are being sent to a more receptive audience.

- They are more cost-efficient than a printed newsletter because of the significant savings in time, printing, and mailing costs.

A patient newsletter demonstrates your concern for the people your practice serves and aims to strengthen that relationship. It is a convenient and impressive way to keep in touch on a regular basis, especially with patients you may not see often.

Collecting email addresses

If you do not have email addresses in your practice management software, I suggest that staff start phoning patients and gathering email addresses. Start with patients who have been into the clinic in the last six months, then those who have visited between six and twelve months ago, then twelve to eighteen months, etc.

Go through your practice management software and extract patient lists for your practice manager/receptionist. Get them to go through this list at the times when the practice is quiet.

Have a script for the caller to follow. For example:

'Hello, this is xxxx from xxxx,

I'm phoning to let you know that we'll be launching some special offers over the coming months and would love to be able to send you the details.

Please can I get your email address so that I can add it to our database? That way we can ensure that you'll be able to take advantage of these offers.'

Please also assure them that you will not be selling their email address and you will only use this email address to provide special offers and information that you believe will be of interest to them.

Sending printed newsletters

A well-produced, printed newsletter still has a place in today's online world. They are a great way to keep your patients informed of new services, treatments, and any special offers available. Sent out twice yearly or quarterly, they are an economical way to communicate quite a large amount of information.

Print newsletters stand out as the more successful of the two types in terms of response rate. When done well, they can generate a good overall return on investment.

The benefits of print newsletters include the following:

- **The mail gets delivered** – It's never blocked by or caught in spam filters. Faulty connections, email authentication, and webmail service idiosyncrasies are not issues. You have no worries about connection speed.

- **They have more perceived value** – Your patients understand the energy, cost, and time required to send them a great practice newsletter. It will get their immediate attention.

- **They let you use an unlimited amount of images** – A picture really is worth a thousand words. Print newsletters are not shackled by bandwidth. That means you can use a variety of text, graphics, and formatting styles to capture the interest of your patients.

- **Print newsletters are portable** – This means that they are more likely to be read.

- **They offer convenient and comfortable reading** – Print newsletters are much easier on the eyes.

- **They stand out and get noticed** – By using colour, logos, and a familiar return address, a print newsletter is easy to spot. With an email inbox filled with subject lines, messages can look the same.

Tips for a great print newsletter:

- Make it visually appealing (use a professional designer).

- Break up the text with some great images. (Professional images are important for profile shots. Good 'self shots' for social news are fine.)

- Use easy-to-understand language. Remember, this is for your patients, not your peers. Try to stick to short words, short sentences, and short paragraphs. Write in the active voice.

- Make the text easy and interesting to read by using techniques like bullet points, italics, bold, and underlining.

- Include a call to action. What do you want your patients to do after reading your newsletter?

- Present an offer or incentive.

The more awareness you build, the more success you will experience! Place copies in your front desk reception area. Post a copy in each consultation room, and put a link to a digital copy on your website. In your waiting room, keep magazines to a minimum.

Leverage non-competing business relationships to share more newsletters, e.g. beauty salons, doctors, lawyers, etc.

Print or email newsletters?

So which is better – email or print newsletters? Print newsletters have more influence but can only be sent periodically. They are more expensive to produce, but they tend to generate a better response rate. Meanwhile, email newsletters are cheaper to send and can be sent more frequently, but they are easier to ignore and tend to generate a lower response rate.

For most practices, the answer is to use both. The delivery mediums are different, and each type of newsletter has its unique virtues. When you work them in tandem, you build powerful brand recognition. Your regular email newsletters supplement your periodic print newsletters, which, in turn, lend credibility to your email newsletters.

You can even offer your patients a choice of subscription. They will see that you really care about what they want, not just what you are able to provide for them.

Social media

Many of your patients can be found on social media these days – the old, the new, and the lost. This makes social media the perfect place to remind them who you are, engage them with information that will benefit them, offer special promotions, explain your services, and make it very simple to request an appointment.

You can use social media for reactivation purposes to establish, maintain, and optimise your practice marketing.

Birthday and thank you cards

Very few dentists use thank you or birthday cards. If you take the time to write cards to your patients, they will see that you are both caring and professional. At the very least, they'll remember the fact that you sent the card, and you'll be on their mind if there's ever a referral opportunity or a chance that they need your services again.

Here are some instances where it would be ideal to send a card:

- When a new patient comes in for a consultation or procedure.
- When a patient refers another patient to you.
- When a patient joins your dental payment club or spends a certain dollar amount with you.
- When it's their birthday.
- When they have a baby.

There are online services such as Send Out Cards and Moonpig that allow you to send physical cards in the mail. Some even have your handwriting copied so that the card looks like you wrote it yourself. These services are great, but a handwritten card, signed by the dentist, is most effective.

Holding a dental open house event

In my opinion, there is really no more friendly way to say thank you to your existing patients and hello to your future patients than to open your doors up wide and invite them in. This is a wonderful opportunity to reach unlimited members of the dental community.

Your open house gives you the opportunity to make connections in a casual and relaxed atmosphere, when you and your staff are not busy doing your day job.

When you might hold an open house:

- Annually.
- To show off a new premises or refurbishment.
- During the school holidays, as a children's event.
- When the practice is under new management or has a significant change in new practitioners.
- For a special anniversary (e.g. ten years in business).

Think about the following elements:

1. Audience

Determining the target audience for your open house should be your first priority. Is it all of your patient base or a specific group?

- Professionals/specialists.
- Community (local businesses/non-patients).
- Parents and families.
- People over a certain age who may be interested in implants.

You may also wish to invite referring specialists, local businesses, and well-known people in your area. Through word of mouth, your practice may benefit from impressing community figures as well as local families.

2. Date and time

Every open house should offer guests a window of time to drop in and visit. A two to three hour window enables patients to visit your practice at their leisure. Weekends, late afternoons, and early evenings after normal business hours are good times to choose for an open house because fewer people will have conflicts with work.

3. Advertising

Once you set the date for your open house, you need to think about how you are going to get people there.

You should post signs in your office to draw patients' interest. Let them know they are welcome to bring family and friends.

- Inform employees. (Make sure the entire team is on board with the event and talking about it.)
- Call your patients personally and let them know.
- Within your practice, post posters and flyers or even a banner on your building.
- Ask current patients to bring a friend for a prize.
- Post on social media.
- Give notice via your recall system and billing statements.

- Invite local press – they are always looking for event news.

- Post on your website.

- Give notice in your newsletter.

- Send emails.

- Approach online local news sites.

- Post in local chambers.

- Display in local businesses (library, council, day cares, salons, restaurants, schools, etc.).

4. Special promotion

Think about what services you plan to highlight at your open house and you can add them to your invitations. Think about promoting a patient special for that day and schedule patients during the event. Think about your ideal patient and what services you are trying to promote and grow within your practice.

In preparation for the event, discuss with your team topics and displays for each of the rooms that would educate and highlight the technology and services that you offer.

5. On-site health seminars

You may wish to hold free seminars on the day that demonstrate the importance of oral health, e.g. a tutorial on proper brushing for small children, a healthy snacks seminar talking about what foods are good for your teeth, a talk on implants, etc. Link these seminars to the services you are promoting.

6. Cross-marketing opportunities

An open house is a perfect opportunity to team up with local businesses such as hair or beauty salons, specialist practices, restaurants, etc. Ask them to advertise your event at their place of business and in return display a thank you and provide an area where they can display their business information at your practice on the day. They may also wish to contribute a prize for a giveaway.

7. Give-away

Everybody loves to leave with a giveaway. Give all attendees a gift bag with branded promotional items, practice information, and a welcome letter or flyer. Remember to include information about your practice, services offered, special offers, and a thank you for coming in.

8. Draw/raffle for prizes

Having a draw or raffle allows you to collect the names and contact information of the guests. Be sure to gather names, addresses, emails, and phone numbers.

Prize ideas:

- Electric toothbrush
- Teeth whitening treatment
- Gift basket
- A prize from a local business, e.g. a meal or a massage, etc.

Remember that any competition is subject to your individual state's laws. Speak to your marketing consultant to ensure that your draw fits with your state laws and legislation.

9. Activities

Have some children's activities available. Great ideas are face painting, balloon twisting and a lucky dip.

10. Food and drink

Have a selection of drinks, finger food, and snacks available. You may even wish to get a local restaurant, business, or caterer to donate food and beverages in return for being able to promote their business at the event and on advertising.

11. Call to action/community support

By adding a charitable element, patients will not only see your practice but also what you stand for and care about. Identify a local charity to support and see what they need and how you could help.

Examples could be to collect donations such as food, books, clothes, or toys. Or you could focus on the health side of dentistry and offer complementary oral cancer screenings.

A wonderful idea is to hold a smile makeover contest. This is where everyone who attends your open house has the opportunity to submit a story about themselves or someone they know who truly deserves a free smile makeover. Not only is this a life-changing prize for someone in the community, it's great for media coverage. You get to experience the difference you can make in someone's life by giving them a smile.

12. *After the event*

What you do after the event is critical. You have spent a significant amount of time, money, and energy, and now it's time to follow up.

- Send thank you notes to all of your guests and any businesses that participated in the event.

- Call prize-winners to come in to the office and collect their gift. Make sure you take their picture to display on social media and in your newsletters (remember to get approval).

- Send a follow-up article and pictures to the local paper.

- Post pictures of the event on social media sites.

- Include the story in your newsletters.

Case study

I was recently invited to an open house with a difference. A local dental practice had decided to hold an event at their local art-house cinema and have an exclusive showing of *That Sugar Film*. This was a free event for the practice patients, their friends, and the community.

They invited a local well-known and highly-regarded health speaker to come along to give an introductory speech.

They had thought of everything. They had:

- Invited their patient base by phone, email, and letter.

- Sent a press release to the local papers.

• Publicised the event on social media.

At the event they had practice goodie bags for all attendees, a selection of healthy sugar-free snacks, promotions, and even a sponsored lucky door prize.

The night was amazing. The practice's profile as a local, caring business was raised to an even higher level.

After the event they had photos and quotes on their social media accounts, in newsletters, and on their website. They sent promotional reminders and follow-ups to all attendees and have now increased their patient base, social media following, and reputation significantly.

On-hold messaging

As you would imagine, I spend a lot of time on hold waiting to speak to dentists about their marketing. It continues to amaze me that there are so many practices who do not use on-hold messages. If you don't have one, you are missing out on a great opportunity to educate your patients about the services that you offer.

Surveys have shown that:[30]

- 70% of all callers are placed on hold.

- Average on-hold time is one minute.

- 90% of callers prefer informative messages to silence or the radio.

On-hold messaging ideas

On-hold time is a great opportunity to offer treatment options and ideas. Some ideas for what to include in your message:

- Talk about your products and services.

- Promote any specials.

- Talk about any new services or techniques.

- Reinforce your branding strategy and positioning statements.

- Address your ideal patient's concerns or fears.

- Tell them more about your practice mission and your vision.

- Inform them about your office hours and days in the office.

- Present your scheduling and appointment policy.

- Promote how to reach your dental office online, including on social media.

- Introduce them to the dentist, associate, or team member of the month.

- Help patients prepare for your appointment.

- Inform them about upcoming promotions, patient events, and marketing events.

On-hold messaging tips

Whatever you decide to include in your on-hold message, it must include the following essential elements:

- Your message must attract.

- It should be informative.

- It should always include a call to action.

Maximising recalls

An effective recall procedure is the best way to keep patients attending regularly. This obviously needs to run alongside educating your patients on the importance of visiting regularly. Recall is one of the most important systems that you can organise in your practice.

Successful recall systems require your practice to employ the right systems and communication channels with patients, and it will require your whole team to be on board with the same message.

The key to a successful continuing care program is to make sure that it is a routine task, just like putting through payments. It is too easy for patients to fall through the cracks. Most patients do not keep up with their continuing care due dates. However, most treatment is scheduled following a recall appointment. This is why it is crucial to make sure that your recall system is solid.

Recall best practice

An effective recall system is critical to running any successful practice. Surprisingly few practices have any type of effective process in place and many allow patients to fall down the 'recall hole'. The more effectively you remind your patients, the less they will put off their care.

The best way is to use multiple forms of communication, e.g. SMS, post, and phone call. Studies show that, historically, a recall system based on one communication with patients would be likely to result in 50% effectiveness whereas sending three recall messages each using different media can result in recall effectiveness as high as 85%.[31]

Paper-based recalls is the commonly used method, yet text messaging is an incredibly effective way to communicate with your patients concerning recalls. Think about it, most people who receive a text read it pretty much instantly.

Practice management software and recalls

There are some great practice management software packages that can fully automate your recall and reminder systems. By using software automation, you can achieve high success rates as the automation removes the reliance on your team, leaving them to spend more time communicating personally with your patients.

It is important for your practice management software to include a recall system that your staff can understand and use. Contact your practice management software supplier and see if you can arrange some time with a consultant to learn and set up your software to maximise its recall functionality.

Monitor your recalls

Examining your recall rates is a really important measure for your dental business.

Use recalls to market your practice

Recalls are another opportunity for you to market to your patients. Don't just send the recall, add in a marketing message. Include some collateral in the envelope with your recall reminder, on the card, or in the text message.

Incentive-based marketing

People are procrastinators; particularly when it comes to dentistry, they need a reason to come back in to see you. Incentive-based marketing is a great way to get your patients to come back in.

Promotions work. The statistics show this, with more than 81% of Australian consumers having purchased a product because of a promotional offer, and almost 40% having done so in the past thirty days.[32]

By using the right promotions, you can retain existing patients, attract new patients, and sell a wider array of services to patients who have traditionally participated in a very small segment of what you offer. Incentives can help you leverage the power of referral-based marketing, too. More practices than ever are using this strategy to drive growth.

Planning your promotions

When thinking about what promotions and incentives you are going to have, think about:

- What you are trying to achieve.

- What your goals are for the promotion.

- What your budget is to run the promotion.

- What systems you have in place to track the conversion and ROI of the promotion.

Promotion ideas

There are many ways you can incentivise people to deal with you rather than another dental practice:

- Give away a low cost item or procedure to incentivise a larger procedure.

- Offer discounts to new patients.

- Offer referral incentives to existing patients who bring you new business.

I don't generally recommend that you discount on a patient's treatment plan but you may wish to offer a gift as an incentive to accept the treatment.

Promoting your incentives

The key to making your incentives as successful as possible is to publicise them as widely as possible. You may have the most amazing promotions in place but if nobody knows about them, what is the point? You need to publicise them and market them across as many of your patient touch points as possible:

- On social media.

- On your website.

- In your email newsletters.

- In your practice (have posters and postcards in your practice).

- In a mailed letter or postcard.

- In a phone call to patients telling them about a promotion and what it means to them.

Most importantly, all of your staff need to know and understand the promotions that you are running and they need to be talking about them to all of the patients they come into contact with.

Tracking your promotions

As with all marketing campaigns, it is critical to track your promotions. Did they convert? What was the ROI of each campaign? Did people understand the campaign clearly or did they ask lots of questions that you had to answer?

I guarantee that some of the promotions will not convert and some of them will. You need to know which promotions to run again, which ones you need to tweak, and which ones to cease. Without tracking, how will you ever know?

As part of judging the success or failure of a promotion, you need to analyse the people that your promotion attracts. Did the patient that was attracted by the promotion stay or just come in for that one procedure, never to be seen again? All promotions need to be focused on attracting and retaining your ideal patient.

Terms and conditions

You also need to clearly specify the terms and conditions of all promotions in accordance with the Dental Board of Australia/ AHPRA guidelines (see Resources) and the relevant Federal, state and territory legislation that applies to your practice. Speak to your marketing consultant to ensure that your terms and conditions comply.

Incentive Marketing Example

An example of how you can use incentive marketing is to encourage people to come in who have outstanding treatments.

If you look in your practice management software, you will probably find a large number of people who have a treatment plan that includes a high priced treatment such as a crown or an implant. These patients know that they need to have this procedure but have been putting it off for many reasons and need a compelling reason to come in.

I recommend that you identify the months in your calendar when you are traditionally quiet. To find this out, go through your previous years' bookings in your practice management software and pick a month that has usually been quiet for you. Then:

- Decide on a procedure that you are going to promote (e.g. implants).

- Decide on a promotion – think of something to give away with that treatment (such as a free sonic toothbrush or take-home teeth-whitening kit).

- Decide on the period of time (e.g. one month).

- Go through and find the patients with this procedure on their treatment plan and promote this offer in as many ways as you can (phone, email, SMS, email newsletter, social media, letters or postcards).

This will give people a compelling reason to pick up the phone and to book in. Each toothbrush may cost you $100, but you are delivering a $2,000 procedure in a month that is traditionally quiet for you.

Step 5 – Checklist

	YES	NO
Do you understand the value of patient retention?	○	○
Do you understand why patients leave?	○	○
Do you have a list of internal marketing strategies to be used for your practice?	○	○
Are you sending newsletters (email or print)?	○	○
Are you engaging in social media?	○	○
Are you sending out birthday and thank you cards?	○	○
Do you hold open house events?	○	○
Do you have effective and targeted on-hold messaging?	○	○
Are you maximising your recalls?	○	○
Are you carrying out any incentive-based marketing?	○	○

Bonus Material

To download checklists and documents
that accompany this book:

Go to www.fullybookeddentist.com/resources

Step 6: Maximise Your Patient Referrals

The value of patient referrals

The best patients have always and will always come through word of mouth. You've probably seen this in your practice for many years. It has been and always will be the best way to grow your business.

'Always give without remembering and always receive without forgetting.'
Brian Tracy

The American Dental Association reports that 70 to 80% of new patients in a typical dental practice are referred by current patients.[33]

People take their health very seriously nowadays. A recommendation from someone they know and trust can make them comfortable about seeking you out as a new medical provider. This is where a referral program can greatly benefit your practice.

Starting a referral program

A referral program (also known as word-of-mouth marketing) entails having some formal procedure in place to motivate your existing patients to refer their friends, family, and colleagues to your practice. Its aim is to make your practice top of mind when patients are talking to their new neighbour or workmate. You need to have a formalised referral program that rewards and recognises patients for referring business to you. A successful referral program increases your average patient lifetime value.

Many happy patients fail to actively refer others to a practice once they leave their appointment. They just don't think about it.

For a successful referral program:

- It needs to be front of mind when patients are in your practice. (Think about having posters on all the walls talking about your program, or a white board saying thank you to the patients who have referred to you, with a list of their names and what they received as a thanks.)

- It needs to be front of mind when patients leave your practice. (Consider giving them referral cards to keep in their pocket or handbag.)

- It needs to be front of mind when patients receive any form of communication from you. (Ensure reminders and emails mention the benefits of making referrals.)

How many referrals should you aim for?

In today's economy, dental practices should aspire to have 40% of existing patients refer at least one new patient per year. Go back and review your records to determine the percentage of patients who have referred another patient in the last twelve months. Are you even tracking this?

Meeting this target will help ensure a healthy increase in hygiene appointments and overall practice revenue. A referral program could be one of the best investments that you ever make.

Securing referrals requires compelling internal marketing. Remember that this type of marketing targets the dental practice's current patients and is less expensive and more effective than external marketing.

Setting your goals

Sit down with your team and set some referral targets. How many referrals would you like to gain every month/every quarter/every year? Make this fun and set a reward such as a meal out or a day out of the practice if the team hits their referral target for the period.

Selecting referral gifts

I recommend that you give people a choice of three gifts. Think non-dental gifts as well as dental gifts. I encourage you to think about the specific demographic of your patients and what you think would appeal to them.

Contact local businesses to work out reciprocal referral deals or discounts. Local businesses are also always looking at innovative ways to get more customers and many would be very interested in offering discounts or free offers to your patients.

When talking to the local businesses, see if you can negotiate to pay them when any vouchers have been redeemed. Studies estimate that 50% of vouchers will not be redeemed.[34]

Referral gift ideas include:

- Movie tickets

- Meal vouchers for a local restaurant

- Massage vouchers for a local spa

- Take-home whitening treatments

- Electronic toothbrushes

I also often see discounts on procedures or an offer of credit ($25 or $50) to the account of the referring patient or new patient. I do not recommend solely using this approach, as I don't think that this has the same pull as the above. People generally don't want money off their dentistry work. They want a gift.

You may also want to have an additional 'grand prize' for referring patients. Each referral that someone brings in gives him or her one entry into the prize draw. You can draw a name on a quarterly basis.

Note that with any kind of grand prize draw, you will be affected by the gaming laws in your state. You need to specify the terms and conditions of any competition/promotion in accordance to the Dental Board of Australia/AHPRA guidelines (see Resources). Speak to your marketing consultant to ensure that your promotion fits with your state laws and legislation.

Promoting your referral program

Once you have a program, it is incredibly important to advertise it to your existing patients.

In the practice:

- Have staff telling everybody and wearing badges.
- Put up posters in the waiting room and throughout the practice (even in the toilet).
- Print referral postcards to hand out to every patient.
- Have a referral program brochure.
- Display referral thank you whiteboards in the waiting room and/ or messages of appreciation on any LCD screens in the practice.
- Mention the program during follow-up phone calls to patients after treatments.
- Include a note with reminders.

Online:

- Have a dedicated referral page on your website.
- Mention the program in newsletters.
- Promote through social media.
- Employ Facebook adverts.
- Make a YouTube video.

Educating staff

The reality for any program in your practice is that it won't succeed unless your staff are on board and understand its importance. You need to take the time to educate your staff on the importance of referrals.

Your practice members interact with patients at every step. This gives them so many opportunities to encourage referrals. Every patient that leaves your practice should be leaving with a clear understanding of your referral program and some referral cards in their hands to give to their family and friends. Your staff should be encouraged to make sure that this happens, and be motivated with targets and rewards.

Remember, the job of the referral program is to bring new enquiries into your practice. It is then the job of the practice staff to convert these new patients into frequent visitors, winning them over with friendly service and educating them on other services that you can offer.

Saying thank you

Once a referral is made, it is incredibly important to follow through. The referring patient (and/or new patient) should receive any gift promised within two to three working days of the referral coming in.

Have a thank you whiteboard in your practice reception or put acknowledgements up on your waiting room LCD screen. Include the patients' names in the referral thank you section of your practice newsletter (with permission).

Remembering the human side

If you want to take your referral program to a whole new level, remember that gifts and acknowledgements are a great place to start, but a personalised thank you is priceless. Make time to do the following:

- Send handwritten thank you notes to referring patients.

- Send handwritten welcome notes to new patients.

- Get the practice principal to call patients who refer others to thank them personally; this will inspire them to refer again.

Tracking referrals

It is incredibly important to have a system in place to track your referrals. You need to have a monitoring system in place for you to know if your marketing dollars are being effective. If your administrative team isn't tracking referral sources, then you can't make smart decisions and you won't know if you are on track to hit your targets. Ensure that:

- You are using systems that are tracking your referrals.

- Your team are trained on how to implement this.

- You ask all new patients how they heard about you.

- You perform spot checks on your data entry systems to check that record keeping is up to scratch.

Case study

I was recently talking to a frustrated practice manager. She told me that their practice 'kind of' has a referral program in place. I asked her to explain. She told me that they started a program where people who referred were meant to receive two movie tickets. She then went on to tell me that the practice principal often didn't follow through on this and didn't give out the movie tickets to the patients that referred!

She said that the reason for this was his opinion that the referrals into the practice didn't convert into enough business to 'warrant' the movie tickets, sometimes not coming back to the practice after their initial visit.

The practice was, therefore, totally inconsistent with their messaging, breaking a promise with their existing patients, and under the impression that the referring patient should be penalised if their referral didn't return to the practice.

If you want your referral program to flourish, you should be consistent and have your program goals understood and agreed upon with your team.

Please note

The legislation regarding referral programs differs by state and territory. Please conduct research and obtain advice on the relevant Federal, state and territory legislation that applies to your practice.

Step 6 – Checklist

	YES	NO
Do you understand the true value of patient referrals?	○	○
Do you have a referral program?	○	○
Do you have goals for your referral program?	○	○
Have you selected the referral gifts?	○	○
Have you told your staff about your referral program?	○	○
Do you have processes in place to promote your referral program?	○	○
Are you tracking your referrals?	○	○

Bonus Material

To download checklists and documents
that accompany this book:

Go to www.fullybookeddentist.com/resources

Step 7: Foster Partnerships And Raise Your Profile

The power of networking and partnerships

An important aspect of marketing your dental practice that is often overlooked or seen as too difficult is to build up a business network within your local community. There can be an advantage to building up this local network. This is where you need to position yourself as both a business owner and a healthcare provider and look for opportunities where you can maximise your position in your local community.

The business of business is relationships; the business of life is human connection.

Robin S. Sharma

Before you launch your community-networking plan, it is important to look again at your ideal patient and review your core values. Think about what you will represent in the minds of your future patients and what benefits you will offer them.

Knowing the right people can get you places that you might not reach otherwise. Creating a network of referring business people (both within and outside of healthcare) could make a huge difference to your business. There are many opportunities for you to get your name out there, it just takes a little thought and effort.

Networking and introducing yourself and your business to strangers soon teaches you the best way to get your message across. At first it can be very hard, but practice and familiarity soon make it second nature. I have seen some people transform from shy beginners to confident crowd-players as their experience builds.

Networking groups

All around Australia there are groups of business owners meeting on a regular basis. Some are small networking groups meeting for breakfast weekly, others are larger organisations that meet on a monthly basis for dinners or seminars. If done well, these groups can be a gold mine of information and referrals that can help you with your business.

The primary reason to attend a networking group is to drive word-of-mouth recommendations. The more people you know who know what you do, the more recommendations you will get. As you know, successful businesses are built on referrals.

Networking is also a great way to find the best suppliers and to build relationships. Whatever sort of supplier you are looking for, whether it is an accountant, printer, recruiter, or insurance broker, you will come across them in your networks. Finding local suppliers that network often provides opportunities for two-way business. You may also want to think about making an offer for referrals through these sources, such as a complimentary consultation.

Meeting other business people and talking about business is a fantastic way of learning new ways to do business. Every business is different and all business people have their own ideas. Finding out how people in other industries, in other markets, and with different services, helps you to generate new ideas and perhaps adapt other people's innovations to your own business.

I recommended that you visit a number of groups that spark your interest. Notice the tone and attitude of the group. Do the people sound supportive of one another? Does the leader appear competent? Many groups will allow you to visit a couple of times before joining.

Networking with other healthcare professionals

I am not suggesting that you start your own healthcare networking group (although some people have). I am recommending that you start networking with other healthcare professionals in your area. This may mean a breakfast or coffee appointment with the GPs in your catchment. This is about increasing your reach. If you have a network of trusted medical professionals, they can be talking to their patients about you and your services.

Professional association membership and association meetings

I strongly recommend that you become an active member of the professional association(s) relating to your speciality. One of the great benefits of belonging to and becoming an active member of a professional association is the opportunity to meet with colleagues working in similar environments with similar challenges.

Being an active member of a professional association allows you to benefit by learning from the experiences of others, continue your education through participation in seminars or workshops, and keep abreast of developments or trends in your industry.

A key reason for involvement with your professional association is networking opportunities. Participation provides the opportunity for you to be recognised in your field and noted for your skills, or it may provide the opportunity to get connected with key people in companies or organisations.

There are many opportunities to raise your profile within these associations such as contributing articles to the newsletters and journals, speaking on a topic of interest, participating on a board of directors or on committees for special projects, and volunteering to assist with meeting coordination or fundraising. All these opportunities can produce both substantial business rewards and great personal satisfaction.

Community involvement

Community involvement should be part of your practice's overall marketing strategy. Community involvement is not the same thing as community advertising. And a successful practice should find a balance and be using a combination of both.

There are numerous benefits to engaging in community service events, not least the benefit of being able to support and help people in your community and give back. Philanthropy can also provide a great opportunity for dental practice marketing.

Getting your practice's name out in the community as a regular participant in locally organised community service events will serve as a form of marketing in itself. The positive associations can be tremendous towards acquiring new patients or retaining existing ones for a dental practice. Being involved in your community can be a fun and rewarding way to not only build your practice, but also to develop team spirit at your office.

Popular ideas are:

- Presentations at local kindergartens and schools.
- Supporting local charities.
- Sponsoring school or community sports teams.
- Chamber of Commerce participation and local business support.
- Exhibiting at local fairs.
- Local service opportunities (e.g. Dental Rescue Day).

Being widely known and recognised in your community will ensure that your practice is on the top of potential patients' lists when they are in need of dental services. Start small so that you can manage things without getting overwhelmed. Make it fun and don't be afraid to try something different.

Volunteering opportunities

Volunteering at a dental event is a way to give back to your community, build your resume, and network with other dental professionals. There are a huge number of organisations in Australia that you can volunteer with. Think about dental organisations for Australia-wide networking or look at local charities to build your local network.

A list of volunteer organisations can be found in the Resources section.

Hosting an event

Using your newsletter as an invitation, hold an event for your loyal patients and encourage them to bring friends. When their friends come to the event, take the opportunity to network and turn those friends into loyal patients.

Running charity promotions

In select issues of your newsletters, cross-promote with charities. By donating space in your newsletter, you show patients that you are a caring, community-oriented professional, an additional reason for patients to trust, remember, and recommend you to their friends. This also gives you an opportunity to offer a portion of patients' dental fees to a charity, enticing them to choose you over dentists not offering the same promotion. Finally, you can use this as an opportunity to sponsor community events and spread your name.

Networking tips

- Ask yourself what your goals are in participating in networking meetings so that you will pick groups that will help you get what you are looking for. Some meetings are based more on learning, making contacts, and/or volunteering rather than on strictly making business connections.

- Have a clear understanding of what you do and why, for whom, and what makes you special or different from others doing the same thing. In order to get referrals, you must first have a clear understanding of what you do so that you can easily articulate it to others.

- Be able to express what you are looking for and how others may help you. Too often people in conversations ask, 'How can I help you?' and no immediate answer comes to mind.

- Follow through quickly and efficiently on referrals you are given. When people give you referrals, your actions are a reflection on them. Respect and honour that and your referrals will grow.

- Call those you meet who may benefit from what you do and vice versa. Express that you enjoyed meeting them, and ask if you could get together and share ideas.

Online networks

LinkedIn is highly focused on forming professional connections. Be sure to keep both your practice LinkedIn profile up-to-date with all of the necessary professional biographical information, and always keep your postings professional.

Staying in touch

Once you've gained access to a contact within an organisation, make a point to stay in touch with them on a consistent basis. It's a good idea to ask your contact how often and by what means they prefer you to stay in touch.

Professional referral marketing

Marketing to referring practitioners and practices is a part of an overall marketing plan for some. This is a critical point for specialised practices, e.g. endodontics, periodontistry, etc. For specialists, referrals from other practices are a major revenue stream.

Like external and internal marketing, taking your message to referring practices requires an organised program with ongoing nurturing. If it's appropriate to your specialty and practice, it will likely be in addition to and not instead of external and internal marketing.

Go about it in the following way:

- Think of about ten people that you know, whom you can phone, who may be able to supply you with patients. This is far more cost effective than advertising in magazines and newspapers. Some of these people might be GPs, therapists who are offering a different service to you, bookshop owners, etc. Schedule a meeting or two every week.

- Write and practice a thirty-second introduction. Tell them the benefits of forming a partnership with you. Tell them a story.

- Keep in touch with this network by sending them information that would interest them. If you read a study or article that would be helpful to them, make copies and send them out with personal notes that say, 'I thought you might be interested'. It takes very little time but it keeps a dialogue going.

- Send them your newsletter. Keep it short and informative and tell them about special offers, the new things you are doing, case studies, and success stories. (Remember, if you are doing this by email, they need to be able to unsubscribe.)

- If you have a special interest and you are a reasonably good speaker, offer to give free workshops for appropriate groups in your community.

- Join a peer group or create one. Every dentist needs a trusted group of colleagues for support, problem-solving, and case sharing. As for marketing, dentists who have confidence in each other, help each other with referrals.

Go and visit the businesses in your area and work with them. You can offer services to their patients and they do the same for you. It's almost free advertising, but very effective. The biggest challenge is going out and talking to your fellow business people in your area.

Thanking your referrals

Few of us take the time to thank people enough. Keep a box of thank you cards on your desk. Before you start your day, think of someone you need to thank for a referral, or for a good conversation, or for alerting you to something.

Referral sources sometimes report that they feel like they have dropped someone into a black hole when they make a referral. They complain that they never hear from the dentist again. If appropriate, ask your patient to sign a release so that you can give some feedback to the person who made the referral.

Write or call to provide appropriate follow-up information. If your patient doesn't want you to do this, see if he or she will at least permit you to let the referring agent know that you are now seeing him or her for treatment.

Reciprocity

If you want the local community to support you, it is much easier if the relationship is reciprocal. Your current patients would love to see 'their' dental practice supporting something they believe in or having stake in their community. Consider sponsoring a local school soccer team, gala dinner, fundraiser, or a local fete.

Whatever you do in your free time, trying to do it locally as much as possible to support your community's businesses. Frequent local cafes and restaurants. If you go to a gym or play sport, try to do it in the community near your practice.

It is a relatively low cost way to get in front of your local community and show that you care about them and are giving back.

Recognising referring businesses

Everyone likes to be recognised and your referring business people are no exception. Reaching out to them and/or their family will improve your relationship. Here are four easy ways to recognise your referring healthcare providers:

1. Acknowledge your referring businessperson's accomplishments with a personal handwritten note.

2. Send birthday and Christmas cards with personal messages. (Christmas cards very often get lost in the volume of holiday cards mailed in December. Sending a card in November allows your message to stand out and will differentiate your dental practice in a positive manner.)

3. Learn the personal interests of your referring business owners and inform them, either with a quick email or a phone call, when you read or see something that they may enjoy.

4. Send unique gifts of particular interest to the referring business.

Following these simple steps can make you stand out amongst the sea of dental specialists. Don't make the mistake of thinking that because you are being used as a referral, you don't have to continue to reach out to your referring healthcare practitioners; new dental specialists are looking to gain a network of referring dentists and physicians as well.

Public speaking

The thought of public speaking strikes fear into the hearts of many. I love this quote from Mark Twain: *'There are only two types of speakers in the world. 1. The nervous and 2. Liars.'*

Attracting new patients and getting professional referrals, can result from something as simple as putting on an information evening at your practice to educate local healthcare professionals on your services or on your specific area of specialisation. Or you could even present to peers at CPD training events such as ADX.

> *'What we say is important ...for in most cases the mouth speaks what the heart is full of.'*
>
> Jim Beggs

Successful public speaking can be easier than you think. If you overcome the natural anxiety, speaking is a useful and effective marketing tool for a meaningful connection with professional peers and prospective patients in the community.

Pubic speaking engagements offer a significant opportunity for both self-promotion and personal growth. By public speaking you can:

1. Present yourself as an expert

Public speaking is the perfect way to present yourself as an expert and to enhance your practice's message, reach, and profits.

If you're highly knowledgeable about something, nobody will know about it unless you demonstrate that knowledge. By speaking publicly on topics within your area of expertise, you can position yourself as an authority within your community and industry.

2. Build your knowledge-base and connections

In many cases, a good talk involves a significant amount of participation from the crowd. Attendees might challenge your viewpoints and offer valuable insights that, ultimately, will give you a well-rounded perspective on the topic at hand. If you go into a talk expecting not just to teach but also to learn, you create an opportunity to really engage with the people at the event in a meaningful way.

3. Increase your visibility online and offline

When you speak at an event, the content that you prepare is intellectual property with a value that can stretch beyond the roomful of people in attendance. By recording the talk and posting a video online (e.g. on Vimeo or YouTube) or just sharing the slides (e.g. on SlideShare.com), you take better advantage of the content you've created for your talk by making it accessible to a wider audience.

4. Promote your business by not promoting it

There's a trick to promoting your business by public speaking, and it has a lot to do with not talking about your business. It's especially important to limit your promotion when giving a presentation. If your talk is one long commercial, you will not be asked back and you will not gain new patients. Do not go in for a hard sell.

Say what you do and the name of your company. Include some examples that involve patients, but be very careful not to cross the line into advertising. Be a resource to people. Teach them something new. Leave them wanting more. And make sure to bring your marketing materials and business cards so they can find you later.

Exhibiting at an event

There are many opportunities for you and your practice to showcase your business at local events. These may be local trade shows, community street fairs, or special events that allow for stalls and stands. These can be an ideal way for you to go out and meet the people in your community.

Event evaluation

The first question for any practice considering exhibiting at any event is: 'Why are we doing this?' Answers like 'because we were there last year' or 'because everyone else is there' aren't good enough. You need to evaluate:

- Who attends this show? Is this your ideal patient?
- How many people will be attending?
- Is this a good use of your time and money?
- If you have exhibited at this event in the past, what was the marketing ROI for this (was it a 3:1 return or higher)?

Pre-planning

Having a stand and exhibiting can take a significant amount of time, money, and effort, so plan it carefully. Questions for your team to answer include:

- What will you exhibit?

- What will your ideal patients want to know or see when visiting your stand?

- What do you specifically want to do at this event? E.g. get leads, increase brand awareness, etc.

The answers to these questions will be the basis for your show strategy. Set realistic goals for each show you attend.

Pre-promotion

An important step that is often missed is to let people know that you will be there before the event. Publish a blog post announcing this, share the information on social media, and add it to your newsletters. You may also wish to put an advert in your local newspaper.

Let your existing clients know that you will be at the event, tell them about any offers or gifts. And ask them to bring along any of their friends that they think could be interested in finding out more about the practice.

On your stand

Think about what you can offer or show to bring people to engage with you and your team and not just walk past. You will get many people who just hover at your stand, so create a list of questions that could be used to open a conversation with people.

Think about what you want to tell people at the event. What are the important messages that you want to get across? Also script the answers to standard questions.

Be friendly, be approachable, and be open. People like to talk to warm, friendly people. Try to stay standing for as much of the time as you can and make a rule that your team cannot use their phones while on the stand. There is nothing less friendly than walking past a stand where people are all sitting and looking at their mobile phones.

Connecting with people

Gathering people's details is incredibly important. When taking their information, prepare your new contacts for future connection by telling them that you'll follow up. This also makes you accountable.

There are a variety of ways you can connect with people:

1. Social media

Social media is a good no-pressure platform to slowly nurture your new connections. If you met someone but didn't make any real plans to follow up, this may be a good place to start.

2. Email

Send an email a day or two after the conference. Remind your contact how you met and mention a highlight or two from your conversation. If you can think of anything that might help them (a brochure, link to an informative video, offer of a free visit to talk about a procedure), make sure to send it to them.

3. Telephone

If someone gave you their contact information, expecting you to call to follow up, make sure you do it. They may actually be waiting for you to call.

Follow-up

Prepare materials you will use to follow up. It is important to have everything printed and assembled in advance, thus allowing the follow-up to happen within a day or two of the event. It is inconceivable to spend money to exhibit and not have an effective follow-up system in place.

Equally important is making contact with the prospective patient to confirm receipt of the information, as well as offering any additional materials that might prove helpful.

- Make sure to promptly follow up all contacts.

- Follow through with all planned and promised discounts and special offers.

- Summarise what happened at the event on your social media pages and website.

Case study

I live in Chatswood in NSW and, every year, my local community puts on a huge family Christmas event, 'Carols in the Park'. This year was bigger than normal (they were expecting three thousand people). Imagine my excitement to see that one of the three sponsors of the event was a local orthodontist.

I thought that this was a really clever thing for them to do. It demonstrates how a dentist can use local events to go out and meet the community.

The event sponsorship cost the practice $4000. For this they got huge exposure in the local community:

- Promotion across all event collateral (road banners, websites, event flyers letter-boxed to the local area, electronic direct marketing sent to more than twenty thousand people, social media, event posters).

- Full-page ad in the carols song booklet distributed to attendees at the event.

- Opportunity to host a promotional stall at the event.

- Opportunity to provide branded material at the event, such as branded LED candles.

At the event, the practice did the following incredibly well:

- They had practice information bags to give to every family as they came into the event, which included leaflets and information on the practice, toothbrushes, stickers, and rubbers. They continued to hand these out throughout the event.

- At their stand, along with further information, they had displays of their treatments, branded LED candles, and frisbees to hand out to all of the children. Both the candles and frisbees gave families a reason to come up to their stand and meet the team.

- They had a full-page advert that included an offer of a 50% discount off an initial consultation.

- They were walking around the families handing out their goodies, chatting with everybody, and answering questions.

They did an exceptional job of getting their name and faces out to the community. A very large proportion of the people there will now be familiar with the practice brand and many will have spoken to the team in person. So, in essence, they ticked all the boxes for 'the community getting to know their name'.

However, they also missed a really important aspect of marketing. As I have said, they did a really great job of getting the community to know the name of their practice. But how many names in the community did they get in return? Unfortunately, they didn't gather people's names and contact details. They missed the opportunity to be able to follow up with the many people that stood chatting to them about their children's teeth.

To gather information from people, you need to give them a reason to leave their details with you. You need to offer something they value in return. Examples of this could be to run a competition to win a meal for four in a local family restaurant or to win a family pass to a theme park (or another family attraction).

In addition, they could have asked people to like their Facebook page or, better still, post a photograph on social media. The most 'liked' photograph could win a prize.

In summary

Make sure, when promoting your brand at events, to gather people's details to build the practice's marketing database, and to follow up and stay in touch with them.

Step 7 – Checklist

	YES	NO
Are you networking with other business and healthcare professionals?	◯	◯
Do you have regular community involvement?	◯	◯
Are you volunteering?	◯	◯
Are you maintaining relationships and thanking referrals?	◯	◯
Have you considered public speaking?	◯	◯
Do you exhibit at any events?	◯	◯

Bonus Material

To download checklists and documents
that accompany this book:

Go to www.fullybookeddentist.com/resources

Step 8:
Learn To Listen

The importance of listening

As Richard Branson says, *'You can never have enough feedback and you can never stop learning.'*

There's nothing more effective for improving the quality of your service than listening to your patients. All practices have some weaknesses in service levels that are usually a blind spot to the practice owners.

> *'Your brand is what people say about you when you're not in the room.'*
>
> Jeff Bezos

Patients that have a negative experience at your practice are unlikely to confront you with it unless they are asked. They are much more likely to simply tell others about it and/or just not come back.

Checking the health of your existing patient relationships will have a profound effect on your dental practice success. Ensuring patient satisfaction will not only improve your overall annual patient spend, it will increase the length of time patients stay with your practice and the number of new patient referrals they will send your way. Meanwhile, patient satisfaction indicators will assist you in making fact-based operational decisions based on your patients' preferences.

- Do you know how your patients feel about your staff and services?

- Do you know what's important to your patients?

- Are you responding to negative experiences before patients are posting about them on Google+, Twitter, and Facebook?

- Do you know what type of effect your team's satisfaction has on patient satisfaction?

- Do you know how likely your patients are to refer family and friends to your practice?

- Do you know if patients feel that your fees are reasonable for the service they receive?

- Do you know what improvements they would like or what things you offer they don't like or want?

The key to maximising patient satisfaction and retention in your practice is to have quality control measures in place that can quickly identify weaknesses in service levels so that they can be fixed quickly when they present themselves.

An essential part of these quality control measures should be to regularly survey your patients anonymously. The feedback you receive will help you continually improve your services to more effectively meet the needs of your patients.

Overcoming the fear

You may not want to face it, but it's there. Patients, and often employees, know when there are problems, issues, or concerns. Even the practice owners or managers might know a problem exists but are trying to ignore its presence.

Remember that perception is reality when it comes to patients. Do you know what the perception is of your practice? Patients can feel the pain; they see the symptoms of poor processes, leadership, or quality. The patient may not always be able to give you the exact reason or cause for the problem, but they can pinpoint the symptoms.

Patient feedback won't all be about telling you where you are going wrong. You will also learn about the parts of the practice that are working and praise-worthy. How valuable would it be for you to find out what your patients really love about coming to you and what it is about your staff that makes them want to come back?

How patient surveys improve business

There are countless reasons for surveying your patients. Surveys can lead to you:

- Improving your customer service.

- Addressing staff training requirements.

- Identifying new service requirements.

- Providing better care.

- Creating happier patients.

- Increasing your revenue.

- Establishing a point of difference.

- Reducing patient attrition.

- Improving the lifetime value of a patient.

- Reducing negative word of mouth.

Asking for patient feedback

Sometimes the problem is that practice owners or managers don't know how to go about setting up a feedback process, or that they think that obtaining patient comments will be too expensive or complex. But most often, the barrier to instituting a plan for listening to the patient is simply the fear of what they will hear.

Once there is acceptance of the importance of learning what the patient has to say, the question becomes how to go about it.

Anonymous satisfaction survey benefits

A customer might be more likely to be honest about their experience if they are taking an anonymous survey.

If you wanted to get a gauge of how you are performing as a practice and simply ask a patient what they thought of their experience, you would be unlikely to get honest feedback as, generally, people don't like to be the bearer of bad news or be confrontational.

Allowing patients to fill in anonymous surveys about their experience gives you a chance at getting an honest view of the patient's journey through your practice. It will give you insight into the weaknesses in your service levels and team and an opportunity to fix these patient service leaks. By working on these, you can make your practice stronger and allow it to grow unhindered.

Although it's anonymous, you can also give the option to the patient to add their contact details if they did wish to discuss their feedback.

Survey tips

- Keep your surveys short.

- Generally, keep the number of questions to a maximum of five. Remember, the goal of your survey is to get a response. You're more likely to get a response if you ask two fast questions than if you ask twelve long ones. Studies have shown that shrinking the survey size can improve response rates by 50% or more.[35]

- Keep your questions simple and limit yourself to three types:

  1. Binaries (yes-or-no questions)

  2. Scales (asking patients to rate something from 1-10)

  3. Open-ended questions (requesting succinct explanations of patient satisfaction or disappointment).

A patient survey is more valuable if it includes at least one open-ended question.[36] Ask a simple question like: 'On a scale of 1-5, how satisfied are you with today's visit?' Then compare those results with an open-ended question like: 'Was there anything about today's visit that you found irritating or frustrating? If so, what was it? Please be direct so we can resolve the issue for the future.'

Not only will open-ended questions help you understand what your dental practice does wrong, but you can also use them to find out which problems have the greatest impact on patient satisfaction.

Where to get patient surveys

Patient surveys may be too complicated for a practice to set up on paper or email and send out. Using third party solutions offer considerable advantages:

- Greater response ratios (surveys completed as a ratio of those sent out) and honesty in feedback, as they are seen as offering an enhanced level of confidentiality over those sent by the practice itself.

- Improved response rates where patients are able to answer by iPad or tablet immediately post-appointment.

- Enhanced services like the ability to break down results by time period or clinician in a practice.

Internet surveys

It's very easy to create simple Internet surveys by sending an email through a service like Survey Monkey for a small cost. Have the survey come from you as the practice owner or manager. Offer a sincere appeal for feedback and make sure patients know not only that it's important to you but also why.

The fact that you want to make sure your practice is doing what it should and that you want to get better, will not only result in more thoughtful responses, but in itself will show patients how you value their satisfaction.

Setting up a process to regularly collect feedback is a most valuable strategy. Maybe it's once a year, or once a month, or maybe it's after every transaction. But plan for it, and make it part of your regular routine.

Giving reminders

To maximise the number of completed patient surveys, mention them personally at the end of the patient's visit. Be the first to invite them to critique you. Don't let that first invitation come from the staff or simply in the email or text you send the patient. Tell them, face-to-face, that you'll send an email (or text message) to the patient, asking a few questions about their experience. Tell the patient that you'd love their honest feedback, negative or positive. Also mention if they have the option of responding anonymously.

Send reminders, but do it judiciously. The last thing you want to become is that practice that endlessly emails reminders about customer surveys. There are two steps to the fine art of sending out reminders:

- **Automated** – After the first survey email has been sent, send a reminder after seven days to anyone who has not responded. Seven days later, send a second automated reminder to those who have still not responded.

- **Manual** – If there are still no responses to the two automated reminders, apply the personal touch. Send a personal email.

As always, the goal is to maximise response rates by making it easy. So your reminder emails should always include a permalink in the body of the email. A permalink, in plain English, is a personalised link taking your patient directly to the survey. No signing in, no entering your patient number, no hoops to jump through. The idea is to simplify accessing the survey, thereby increasing the chance you'll get a response.

Giving gifts to encourage survey participation

You may also wish to offer something in return for people completing your survey. Here are a few suggestions:

- **Offer a prize** – I've seen a lot of success combining surveys with a contest, as in 'the person who submits the most interesting answer wins a prize'.

- **Give every participant something** – Do a giveaway for every patient who offers you some feedback in a twenty-four-hour period. This can be a great way to find out what's on patients' minds. These may take a time or money investment, but they are terrific for engaging patients and building their loyalty to your practice.

- **Make a donation to charity** – Offer a list of charities that the patient can choose from (present a range, e.g. children, animals, medical-related) and say that you will make a donation in the name of those who offer feedback.

Note that if you decide to go for a prize incentive, you will be affected by the gaming laws in your state. You also need to specify the terms and conditions of the competition in accordance with the Dental Board of Australia/AHPRA guidelines (see Resources). Speak to your marketing consultant to ensure that your draw fits with your state laws and legislation.

Handling feedback

The way practices handle feedback can mean the difference between success and failure in an increasingly competitive marketplace. Practices that turn complaints into opportunities for building closer relationships with patients are the ones that are most likely to survive and prosper.

A complaint is a signal that should not be ignored. When patients complain, they are giving your practice an opportunity to fix what is wrong and improve. Patients act in their own self-interest, and they are in a unique position to tell your company the unvarnished truth – something your employees are unlikely to do because it might reflect negatively on their performance or they fear that you'll 'shoot the messenger' rather than listen to the message. Just about every comprehensive study done on this subject points to greater success for companies that turn the negatives represented by complaints into positives.

Responding immediately to feedback

Did you know that patients who have their complaint resolved are up to 8% more loyal than if they never had a problem in the first place?[37]

When patients reply, you need to show you're listening. Here's how to do it in three steps:

1. **Thank them.** Show gratitude for any type of response, even if it's not something you can act on.

2. **Acknowledge their specific feedback.** Make it clear that you understand their request and empathise with their needs and expectations.

3. **Share how you're going to act on their feedback.** Be honest. Even if their feedback is something you can't act on, let them know their feedback has been passed to an appropriate team. At the very least, your patient will feel as if their comments were received and processed.

Giving staff objective negative feedback

Giving team members negative feedback can be very uncomfortable. When there are measurable deliverables that haven't been met by a staff member (like turning up to work on time or supplies that haven't been ordered), this feedback is at least objective. But many dentists find it harder to give negative feedback about a team member's patient service as it can be seen by the recipient as just the dentist's subjective view of things. While the recipient of the feedback may nod their head when receiving the feedback, the scale of the problem and its impact on the practice is often in question.

Being able to show negative results from patient surveys is a much easier conversation because the negative feedback and its impact are seen as objective rather than just 'your opinion'. It is much easier to give the negative feedback from the survey because it is the patients' feedback not yours.

Getting employee feedback

Recognise the value of empowering your employees. I recommend using surveys on a regular basis with your patient-facing employees and asking them for their observations when it comes to patient reactions.

Ask them what they think is working, what is not working, and why. This can be a great way to seek new opportunities to increase patient satisfaction.

Listening online

Do you know what your patients are saying about you behind your back? Do you know that your patients are talking about you online, leaving comments and feedback on how you and your staff are doing their job?

> 'Your most unhappy customers are your greatest source of learning.'
>
> Bill Gates

- 90% of customers prefer word of mouth to any other form of marketing for information on services.[38]

- 70% of Australian consumers trust online reviews.[39]

In the past few years, the term 'reputation management' has evolved, but it doesn't refer to what you publish online. Reputation management is defined as overseeing the online reviews about a company or professional. Online reviews are patient testimonials about you or your practice, posted on Google+, Yelp!, Facebook and other review sites.

Are you aware that the new patients you are trying so hard to attract are reading online reviews? 49% of consumers state that they are more likely to visit a business after reading a positive online review.[40]

Quite simply, you need to be watching and listening to what your patients are saying about you online.

What is an online reputation?

This can be defined as the way you are perceived by a random Internet user. It's what they read about you online, what they write about you online, and what they share about you online.

85% of your patients will leave you for what they perceive is a lack of patient service.[41] With Facebook, Twitter, and text messaging, patients can instantly say bad things about your practice. All it takes to earn a patient's disapproval is a lack of common courtesy or inattention to detail.

Remember – potential patients read online reviews.

According to research, over two-thirds of Australians read online reviews before making a purchasing decision.[42] 90% of people believe testimonials from people they know, while 70% believe reviews from people they don't know.

Patients who participate in online conversations usually make a decision during their interaction, and ultimately spend more on a service or product, feeling that they've made an informed decision.

How can a dentist avoid negative online reviews? That's the big question. The answer is you probably can't, so you need reputation management.

Reputation management for dentists

Many review sites allow a business to respond publicly to reviews. This is always a good idea. In the case of positive reviews, respond with a brief statement of appreciation. For negative reviews, respond with compassion and concern. Invite the reviewer to call the practice and speak with you personally. Mention that patient service is very important to you, and that you would appreciate hearing the reviewer's story. Do not get involved in a tit-for-tat. Do not defend your actions. Instead, respond only with kind words and empathy.

What your patients think about you is important but what they share further dictates practice success. You need to ensure that you are kept updated of any mention of you or your business on Yahoo, Google, or Bing. To do this, set up a Google alert for your name, practice name, and associates' names. You will then receive an email every time Google indexes the word or words you identified when setting up the alert.

To set up your Google alerts, go to http://www.google.com.au/alerts.

If you run across a negative review, decide what you'll do to counteract it and then take action.

> ### Online reputation examples
>
> I so often talk to practices who, in their own words, are 'sticking their heads in the sand' and don't want to hear what is being said or written about them. Many know that reviews are happening out there, they just don't want to hear what is being said. When I carry out the searches on their behalf, many are pleasantly surprised to hear what people are saying.
>
> Both types of feedback are a gift to your practice – both positive and negative. How valuable is it to know that you have been marked down in 'time to get an appointment' and how easy for you to look at your systems and work on this?
>
> Some other practices are oblivious to the fact that they are 'out there'. They will quite often say, 'I have no internet presence', only for me to come back and show them twenty-two reviews from their patients. They are staggered because they really had no clue that there was anything written about them.

Online sites you should be watching

There are many websites where people can leave reviews of your practice and the dentists. Here are some of the main ones that you should be watching:

General review websites:

- Your Google+ page – https://plus.google.com
- Your Facebook page – https://www.facebook.com

- Yellow Pages – http://yellowpages.com.au

- Womo – http://www.womo.com.au

- True Local – http://truelocal.com.au

- Yelp – http://www.yelp.com.au/

- Start Local – http://www.startlocal.com.au/health/dentists/

Review websites specifically aimed at reviewing dental and medical fields:

- Whitecoat – https://www.whitecoat.com.au

- RateMd – https://www.ratemds.com

- What Clinic – http://www.whatclinic.com/dentists/australia

Proactive online reputation management

From a practicing dentist's point of view, it makes sense to be proactive in protecting and managing your online reputation. A growing number of patients are inclined to check out a dentist's background online before a first visit. The first challenge for a dentist is to ensure that ratings and review websites maintain the latest information about the practice. Dentists need to know which websites their practice is listed on and provide relevant updates as they happen.

AHPRA Guidelines

At the time of writing, practitioners in Australia are unable to use patient testimonials in any form or promotion or advertising. Therefore, you should not ask or encourage your patients to leave reviews on online review websites. This is due to the guidelines given by the Dental Board of Australia's Australian Health Practitioner Regulation Agency (AHPRA guidelines).

See the Resources section for more information

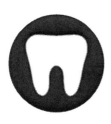

In summary

It can take years to build a positive online reputation, but just one bad review going viral could turn everything you have accomplished upside down. With the growing influence of the Internet, practicing dentists need to take smart steps to build and protect their professional reputation online.

Case study

One client I spoke to recently had been given a huge amount of 5 star ratings from their patients. They then received a 1 star, terrible review saying that they were the worst dentists in their city. The assumption made by the practice team was that the person posting this remark was a jealous competitor (I agreed).

When they searched in their practice management software, he did not exist in their records. When you looked at his Facebook profile, it had no activity except for this one terrible review. Oh yes, and his Facebook profile image was a stock image and not a real photo.

When this happened, the practice owner was obviously and very understandably angry about it and abruptly responded to the 'reviewer' online. The problem with this was that everybody who looked at their Facebook page could also see this remark.

My recommendation with any negative feedback that is received on social media is to respond with honour. Use this as an opportunity to show the world how understanding, caring and thoughtful you are.

In this case, I would recommend a response along the lines of:

Dear xxx

We are so sorry that you have had this terrible experience with a dentist. We have searched our database and we have no record of you ever visiting our practice. We can only assume that you must have made a mistake and confused us with another practice.

At our practice we pride ourselves on our patient care (as the other reviews from patients show) and would never treat our patients the way you described.

Once again, we are sorry to hear that you had this terrible experience with this other practice.

Best wishes

xxx

Step 8 – Checklist

	YES	NO
Do you understand why collecting feedback is important?	◯	◯
Are you asking for and collecting patient feedback?	◯	◯
Are you asking for and collecting staff feedback?	◯	◯
Do you have systems in place to respond to feedback?	◯	◯
Are you watching and responding to online feedback?	◯	◯

Bonus Material

To download checklists and documents
that accompany this book:

Go to www.fullybookeddentist.com/resources

Step 9:
Review, Revise, Retry

Reviewing your marketing strategy

It will take about six months of following your marketing strategy before you can look back and see what's working and what isn't working. After that first six-month waiting period, schedule an evaluation process at least every quarter to keep your marketing on track. There is no point in creating and implementing a marketing plan unless you also track its successes and failures.

> 'The cost of being wrong is less than the cost of doing nothing.'
>
> Seth Godin

There will be elements that are working and elements that aren't. If you get impatient and don't wait long enough to gather your data, you'll be flailing in the dark. This could result in you trying to make changes to something that may not be broken.

During your evaluation process, think about your vision and your marketing goals, as well as your budget and timeline.

- Are you reaching your goals?

- Is the message you are putting out in line with your vision?

- Have you stayed within your budget, and are you meeting your milestones?

- Do you have unified branding across your campaigns?

Evaluate performance against your original plan. If there is poor performance, you will be required to take corrective action to improve the situation. This may involve complete overhaul, changes at a strategic level, or smaller tactical changes.

Marketing strategies can become out-dated as the marketplace changes. Your practice should regularly reassess and modify your marketing programs accordingly.

An important factor to consider when adjusting a marketing campaign is the cost, as well as the difficulties associated with making changes. You will need to assess all of the relevant and hidden costs of changing your campaign. A decision will then have to be made by comparing the possible benefits of making the changes with the costs involved.

Revisiting your marketing goals

The first step in any good marketing strategy evaluation is a thorough examination of the specific goals you have set for yourself in the past.

Take the time to determine whether or not you are hitting your target projections. Revise previous goals based on your current performance and change them as necessary to accommodate new objectives or to account for changes in service offerings.

Checking your marketing ROI

The main thing that you will want to evaluate when it comes to assessing your marketing performance is your overall return on investment (ROI). Calculating your exact returns can be difficult, but you'll ultimately find that the data that you are able to produce is well worth your efforts.

To measure ROI, you will need to track two different variables:

1. The amount that you have invested into your marketing campaigns (account for both financial investments and time expenditures).

2. The financial benefit of any conversions that you are tracking.

As a rough example, imagine that your practice has spent $500 on marketing materials and $500 in labour hours to promote them on social media. Then determine that inbound visitors from social networking websites have accounted for one sale of $200 (total). You can see that you would want to scale back or realign your marketing efforts for this example.

If, on the other hand, you see that visitors from one particular social media website have accounted for 80% of those sales, you may decide to refocus your efforts in order to concentrate on the traffic streams that have proven most valuable to your practice's bottom line.

Re-examining your ideal patient profiles

Re-examine your ideal patient profiles to ensure that your ideal demographic can still be reached through your campaigns and that you're still targeting the right patients for your practice.

Taking a look at your online presence

As you re-examine the types of patients that you want to target, you will also need to periodically assess whether or not you are actively participating on the right online sites and whether your own website and social media platforms are performing.

- How many visitors to your website are you getting?

- How long are they staying on your website?

- How many new 'likes' do you have on social media?

- Are the levels of engagement on social media increasing or decreasing?

- What are your online reviews saying?

- What is the open rate and click through rate on your email newsletters?

- What is your Google ranking?

- How many Google plus reviews do you have?

- How many new posts have you put onto all of your social media platforms?

- How many new blog posts have you published and how many do you have planned for the future?

Evaluating your messaging strategies

Next, take a look at the specific types of message that you are releasing as part of your marketing campaigns. Specifically, evaluate:

- Which types of message (i.e. text-based status updates, blog posts, videos, email newsletters, etc.) are performing best with your audience?

- Are the words chosen for various messaging pieces resonating with your audience?

- How frequently are your marketing materials being shared amongst users?

If your marketing message is in line with your patients' expectations, you will see high levels of engagement with your branded materials, as well as a high number of social shares as people pass your content on to others. If you are not yet seeing these results, this could indicate a mismatch between your practice's messaging and your patients' interests.

Scheduling reviews

The monthly update

A good marketing plan is full of milestones, assumptions and tasks, all of which should be measurable. Make sure you review and update these measured results every month. This can be done within your practice or you may like to bring in your marketing consultant.

For each of the standard campaigns you have in place, you should maintain a table with the plan, another with actual results, and a third with the difference between plan and actual, which is called variance. As an annual plan marches through the months, you can use the table reserved for actual results to include changes in budget that affect the near future.

The quarterly update

This is the perfect time to bring in your marketing consultant, who can go through your ongoing marketing results in detail and make changes to the strategy where necessary.

The annual update

Update your plan thoroughly at least once a year. If you can, get your marketing consultant to come in and do this with you. Start with the previous version of your plan and revise it. But make sure you're taking a fresh look.

Think about the following:

- What new technology, skills, or areas of interest do you have in your practice?

- Do you have new members of staff who can bring in new skills and expand what you can deliver or how you can market?

- What trends have you seen in dentistry in Australia and elsewhere?

- What trends are you seeing in your areas of specialisation?

- Are there changes to your patient demographic?

- What are your competitors doing?

- What are your patients buying? What problems are you solving? What other solutions can they choose? Talk to your patients and potential patients and review your value proposition.

Revising your marketing strategy

After a review of your marketing activities, you may be required to adjust certain marketing campaigns. This may be due to changes in the market or because the campaigns are failing to meet their objectives. In a well-orchestrated marketing program, strategies that do not work are taken out and new ones are put in place.

If a particular campaign is significantly under-performing or it appears that the marketing strategy has failed, it may be necessary to return to the research and planning stage. You can either abandon the campaign altogether, write off the expense, then start fresh with a new campaign, or you might seriously modify the objectives or strategy to try and improve performance. Both have costs that need to be taken into account.

After implementing an adjusted or brand new marketing strategy, it is important to reassess and evaluate the changes after a short period of time. This will allow you to gauge if the results are better, the same, or worse when compared to the previous strategy.

Retry

So often, I see practices that start off strong and then their marketing efforts fade out. Keep it fresh – try new things every month if you can.

How can you keep yourself and your practice focused? This is where a marketing consultant or marketing coach can come in handy.

You may also want to keep regular goals and rewards in place for your team so that they are continually motivated to keep going with your marketing efforts.

Keep your team informed at every point in the process. It is critical to the success of your marketing to have ongoing conversations with your team so that everybody knows what you are trying to achieve and how you are progressing. Open lines of communication are essential for consistent marketing. Make sure the entire team knows where to focus in terms of the revised plan and make sure they understand why an approach may have changed.

Step 9 – Checklist

	YES	NO
Are you reviewing your marketing strategy on a regular basis?	○	○
Do you revisit your marketing goals?	○	○
Are you checking your marketing ROI?	○	○
Have you re-examined your ideal patient profiles?	○	○
Have you re-evaluated your online presence?	○	○
Do you know what messaging strategies are working best for you?	○	○
Are you keeping your team informed?	○	○

Bonus Material

To download checklists and documents that accompany this book:

Go to www.fullybookeddentist.com/resources

Where To From Here?

I hope that you have found *Fully Booked* insightful and helpful. In the understanding that there is no silver bullet, you now know that you need to think about multiple touch points when it comes to marketing your practice. You know that it takes time but the effort that you put in will be rewarded by more patients, increased production, better relationships with your team and patients and a sense of control when it comes to your marketing.

> *'The more that you read, the more things you will know. The more that you learn, the more places you'll go.'*
> Dr Seuss

There is no magic when it comes to successfully marketing your practice. Quite simply, it comes down to:

- Picking the aspects of marketing you want to use wisely and with due care and thought.

- Making sure that whatever marketing activities you decide to undertake you perform to the best of your ability and budget.

- Being consistent.

- Tracking your results – setting your goals and reviewing/refining them on a regular basis.

- Getting good advice from trusted experts in the area of marketing you are undertaking.

It is now time for you to focus on your marketing; do it well, do it consistently, and say goodbye to the scattergun approach forever.

I hope that you can dip into this book over and over again. Use it as a reference before you start to think about any marketing now or in the future. Share it with your team so that they can understand the importance of your marketing campaigns.

My greatest hope for this book is that it can help dental practices improve their marketing game, enabling them to step up and get back in control. Safe in the knowledge that their marketing is well thought out, strategic, and being tracked, dentists can focus on providing amazing dental services to their patients.

If this book saves practices from being cheated by the sharks and cowboys in the website and marketing industry then I have made a difference. When it comes to the dicey providers, I implore you to listen to your intuition and gut feeling. If you are talking to a provider and it 'feels' wrong then it probably is. Stop and get advice before you waste thousands or tens of thousands of dollars.

Take your marketing one step at a time and, most importantly, have fun. What can be better than building strong and profitable relationships with your patients?

I wish you the very best of luck and success.

Carolyn

Let's keep in touch

I would love to hear any feedback you have on the book – what you loved, anything you disliked and any questions that you have. You can stay in touch with me on social media or we may meet at a presentation, training course, or expo some time soon.

'Today is your day, your mountain is waiting. So get on your way.'

Dr Seuss

Contact

Email – carolyn@fullybookeddentist.com

Telephone – 02 9410 1507

International – +61 2 9410 1507

Websites

Fully Booked – www.fullybookeddentist.com

My Dental Marketing – www.mydentalmarketing.com.au

Wellsites – www.wellsites.com.au

Social

Facebook – www.facebook.com/CarolynSDean.Author

LinkedIn – www.linkedin.com/in/carolyndean

Twitter – www.twitter.com/carolyn_dean

Acknowledgements

There are so many people who have helped me achieve what I believed to be unachievable and who continuously support me on my journey, with my rapidly growing business, young family, and generally crazy life.

Firstly, I want to thank all of the incredible dental professionals who have openly and honestly shared personal, professional and financial information with me. Without your honesty I would not have being able to truly understand your businesses, your struggles and worries, and the real challenges you face. Your willingness to share your experiences of the good, the bad and the ugly of dental marketing gave me the insight and drive to write this book. I feel incredibly lucky to be able to speak on a daily basis to so many ethical, caring and intelligent people. I honestly feel like I have the best clients in the world!

My endless thanks to my amazing team at Wellsites and My Dental Marketing (past, present and future) – Katie, Annamaria, Charlie, Cherry, Theresa, Michelle, Renee, Jessie, Sheba, and Kirsten. I am so lucky to be surrounded by such a smart, caring, professional and flexible team. You support me in all of my crazy ideas and always come through and deliver with impeccable results.

You are all living examples of how to deliver great services in the most professional way. I am so proud of what we have achieved together over the years and so excited about what we can do in the future. I cannot thank you enough.

Thank you to all of the people who have given their time to enable me to write this book. To Alvin Low and Anna Low from No Gaps Dental, to Lisa Conway from Maven Dental and to Lynda Hunter from Greenwood Dental for allowing me to interview them directly about their experiences with dental marketing and for giving me the kick-start to begin this book.

To Phillip Palmer from Prime Practice for writing the foreword and for your support and enthusiasm.

To Andrew Griffith, Glen Carlson and the KPI team, I would never have started (let alone finished) this book without your incredible guidance and coaching. To my editor Sara Litchfield, who took a very rough first manuscript and encouraged and guided me to deliver the book – something that I thought at moments might never end! To Gwen Blake and the team at Boxer and Co. for delivering a book cover that was way beyond anything that I could have imagined. To my publisher Michael Hanrahan for taking all of the hard work and confusion regarding publishing away from me and making the whole publishing process smooth and simple. To Ursuala Hogben, Niki Tranfield, Theresa Amos and Katie Sykes for taking the time to proofread my manuscript. To Melinda Leyshon who helped me battle my way through the endless choice of editors and options.

To all of the people in the dental industry who have been so enthusiastic and have taken the time to review and endorse this book – Michael Fahey, Rob Johnson, Dr. Frank Papadopoulos, Jonathan Engle, Abe Awakian, Dr. Andrea Clarke, Ian Shapland, Dr. Sara Lonergan, Albert Gigl, Dr. Jeff Brown, Robert Bowles, Steve Daley, Julie Parker, Dr. Saif Hayek, David Hazlewood and Toni Black.

To the amazing team at Prime Practice, especially Phillip, Wayne, Brett and Anna-Lisa for your ongoing support of My Dental Marketing and of me both personally and professionally.

To my amazing network of incredible female entrepreneurs and the members of the First Seeds Board who are forever supporting each other, celebrating each other's wins and picking each other up if we trip. You are a constant supply of inspiration, support and advice that I could not do without.

To the Journey Girls for your support and love over the last years, especially Penelope aka 'Dr. Nelope' for your endless enthusiasm and encouragement for all of my dental business endeavours.

To my incredible community of neighbours, friends and the parents of JC School who are always available and willing to help me out and support me in any way when it comes to my constant juggle of work and family.

To my wonderful aunt Teresa, who left her own family in the UK for two months to come to Australia to help me with juggling school holidays and book writing!

To Mum and Dad, although we are far away from each other, you are the foundation who made me who I am today. Your constant belief and support in me growing up meant that I was brave enough to constantly try. I always knew that, no matter what I achieved, you would be there for me.

To Tracey, Siobhan, Martin, Megan, Steve, Ben and Matt. We are such a small family but with huge hearts. Although we are half a world away, it means so much to me to know that you are always there for me.

Finally, and most importantly, to Gerry, Callum and Ciara. You are my everything; you are the reason that I live, breathe and keep going. You put up with all of the stress of juggling a business and a family. You constantly support me in everything I do with the greatest understanding and enthusiasm. You are the centre of my universe and I love you all more than words can ever say.

Appendix – Resources

Dental marketing and business books

- *Everything is Marketing: The Ultimate Strategy for Dental Practice Growth* – Fred Joyal

- *Pillars of Dental Success* – Mark A. Costes DDS

- *Marketing The Million Dollar Practice* – Dr. Bill Williams

- *It All Starts with Marketing: 201 Marketing Tips for Growing a Dental Practice* – Dr. Ann Marie Gorczyca

- *Retention: Retention: How to plug the #1 profit leak in your dental practice* – Dr. Jesse Green

- *The Definitive Guide To Dental Practice Success: Time-Tested Secrets to Attract new patients and retain your existing patients* – Jerry Jones

- *How to Get New Dental Patients with the Power of the Website* – Adam Zilko, Jacob Puhl

- *'Valuocity: A Fable for Dentists* – Dr. Marc B. Cooper, Dr. Mark E. Silberg

- *How To Build The Dental Practice Of Your Dreams* – David Moffet

General marketing and business books

- *Unmarketing* – Scott Stratten

- *Delivering Happiness: A Path to Profits, Passion, and Purpose* (Zappos) – Tony Hsieh

- *Permission Marketing: Turning Strangers into Friends and Friends into Patients* – Seth Godin

- *Purple Cow* – Seth Godin

- *Start With Why* – Simon Sinek

- *Good to Great* – Jim Collins

- *The E-Myth Revisited* – Michel Gerber

- *Blue Ocean Strategy* – W. Chan Kim

Consulting, coaching, and training

Dental marketing consulting

- **My Dental Marketing** – http://mydentalmarketing.com.au

Dental business coaching

- **Prime Practice** – https://primepractice.com.au

- **Momentum Management** – http://www.momentummanagement.com.au

- **Julie Parker Dental Management** – http://www.julieparkerdentalmanagement.com.au

- **Dr. Jesse Green** – http://drjessegreen.com

Seminars and CPD training

- **ADA NSW Centre for Professional Development** – https://adacpd.com.au/

- **ADX** – http://ADX.org.au

- **ADA** (events and congress) – http://www.ada.org.au

- **AesthetiCon** – http://www.aadfa.net

Interpersonal skills training

- **Prime Speak** –
  https://primepractice.com.au/workshops/primespeak-seminar

Dental volunteer organisations

- **Kimberley Dental Team** –
  http://www.kimberleydentalteam.com

- **Filling The Gap** – http://www.fillingthegap.com.au

- **National Dental Foundation** –
  http://www.nationaldentalfoundation.org.au/

- **Give A Smile** – http://www.giveasmile.org.au

- **Australian Red Cross Dental Days** –
  http://www.ada.org.au/volunteers/redcrossproject.aspx

Website marketing

We use a number of tools to analyse the performance and usability of websites:

- **Google mobile friendly check** –
  https://www.google.com/webmasters/tools/mobile-friendly/

- **Screen check** – http://quirktools.com/screenfly/

- **SEM Rush** – http://semrush.com

- **Quick Sprout** – http://quicksprout.com

- **Hubspot website grader** – https://marketing.grader.com

Patient surveys

- **Dental Patient Surveys** (run by Prime Practice) – www.dentalpatientsurveys.com

- **Survey monkey** – www.surveymonkey.com

Stock images

Do not fall into the trap of stealing images from other people's websites. Using images that you have not bought or do not belong to you can cause you a lot of problems. I have had clients with court cases and/or hefty fines who have used images that they are not licensed to use.

You need to take your own images or have permission (including buying a license). We recommend the following websites:

Paid stock images

- **Istockphoto** – paid stock images great for websites and other design work http://www.istockphoto.com

- **Shutterstock** – paid stock images great for websites and other design work http://www.shutterstock.com

Free stock images

- **Morguefiles** – free stock images perfect for blog posts and social media http://www.morguefile.com

- **Pixabay** – free stock images perfect for blog posts and social media http://pixabay.com

Social media

- **Google for business (Google+)** – http://www.google.com/business

- **Facebook** – http://facebook.com

- **Twitter** – http://twitter.com

- **Instagram** – http://instagram.com

- **YouTube** – http://youtube.com

- **Pinterest** – http://pinterest.com

- **LinkedIn** – http://linkedin.com

Social media tools

- **Buffer** – provides an easy way to share updates on your social profiles.

- **Hootsuite** – is the ultimate social media management tool for all types of user. It provides an easy-to-use interface to monitor and manage all of your social media profiles from one single dashboard.

- **Google Analytics** – is the most powerful free analytics tool available on the market.

- **Facebook Insights** – gives you a deeper look into how your website is performing on Facebook's platform.

- **Twitter Analytics** – Twitter provides its own analytics to all users. You can see how your tweets are performing, what kind of updates are getting more attention, etc.

- **Pinterest Analytics** – Pinterest also has its own analytics tool, which can help you track your site's performance on Pinterest. You can see the performance of your pins and boards.

- **YouTube Analytics** – If you are a YouTube publisher, then YouTube Analytics is a great tool for you. It gives you detailed insights into how your channel is doing on the YouTube platform.

- **Google Alerts** – Set up Google to notify you by email every time Google indexes the word or words you identified when setting up the alert. https://www.google.com.au/alerts

Advertising and the national law

The advice offered in the book is general marketing advice. Before following this advice you need to check that you are operating within all regulatory frameworks.

Please conduct research and obtain advice on the relevant Federal, state and territory legislation that applies to your practice.

To find the latest versions of the AHPRA Guidelines for advertising regulated health services, go to – http://www.ahpra.gov.au

Appendix – My Dental Marketing Services

About My Dental Marketing

Founded in 2009, My Dental Marketing (formerly Wellsites*) has proven results in supporting dental practices to improve their marketing, attract more patients, and stand out from competitors.

'We believe your practice marketing should never be ad-hoc, but rather part of a larger strategy for business growth and prosperity.'

My Dental Marketing

We are trusted marketing consultants with specialist expertise in the dental industry. My Dental Marketing is passionate about helping dental practices attract and retain patients by delivering focused marketing solutions and consulting to suit a practice's needs. We understand that all practices are different and have different needs, different goals, and a huge range of different experiences behind them when it comes to marketing their practice.

My Dental Marketing and Wellsites have worked with over four hundred dental and medical professionals in Australia, New Zealand, and around the world.

* Wellsites: An award winning specialist in marketing services and website design for dental, medical, and healthcare professionals

Our services

My Dental Marketing is committed to assisting dental practices in using marketing to attract new and keep existing clients. We know that every dental business is unique, so our solutions are developed to best represent your practice in style and affordability.

'Long-term communication with your patients creates a valuable practice brand and builds your revenue.'

My Dental Marketing

These solutions have long-lasting, visible effects on your practice, with updates and modifications to suit your changing environment and to constantly appeal to your patients.

Marketing coaching and consultancy

We have a team of marketing consultants that can work with you and your team throughout the nine-step process detailed in *Fully Booked*. Work with one of our experienced consultants who can answer all of your questions, provide guidance, and share the latest skills and knowledge needed to ensure your marketing is unsurpassed by your competition.

Website design

A well-designed and effective website is the key to successful dental marketing. We understand the very specific online marketing needs of the dental community.

Online marketing services

Once you have your website, you need to ensure that you can be found online. We can provide online marketing services such as SEO, PPC, email marketing, blog writing, and social media services.

Practice branding & identity

Well-considered, professionally-designed dental practice branding instantly communicates your professionalism, competence, and character. We design materials that are a true representation of you and your practice.

Marketing services

We have a comprehensive range of marketing services such as fully customised practice marketing campaigns, marketing planning and strategies, public relations, patient reactivation campaigns, and referral marketing solutions.

> 'Your dental marketing in safe hands.'
>
> My Dental Marketing

Contact us to find out more

- Phone – 02 9410 1507
- Website – www.mydentalmarketing.com.au
- Facebook – www.facebook.com/mydentalmarketing

Appendix – Footnotes

1. Baldwin & Sohal, 2003, "Service quality factors and outcomes in dental care", Managing Service Quality: *An International Journal*, Vol. 13 Iss: 3, pp.207–216

Prime Practice, 2014, "Checking your blind spot", <http://bitemagazine.com.au/checking-your-blind-spot>

RDH eVillage, 2012, "What patients like about dental office experience", <http://www.dentistryiq.com/articles/2012/12/survey-what-do-patients-like-about-dental-offices.html>

2. Donovan, S, 2014, "Australia to have a dentist glut until at least 2025, report finds", <http://www.abc.net.au/am/content/2014/s4151784.htm>

3. Donovan, S, 2014, "Australia to have a dentist glut until at least 2025, report finds", <http://www.abc.net.au/am/content/2014/s4151784.htm>

4. Australian Dental Industry Association, 2014, "The ADIA Dental Industry Business Conditions Survey, May 2014"

5. Software of Excellence, 2014, "Facing the Challenge of New Patient Acquisition"

6. Joyal, F, 2009, "Everything Is Marketing"

7. Wikipedia, "Effective Frequency", <https://en.wikipedia.org/wiki/Effective_frequency>

8. Joyal, F, 2005 "They Didn't Teach This in Dental School", <http://www.1800dentist.com/they-didnt-teach-this-in-dental-school>

9. Nielsen, J, 2010, "Photos as Website Content", <http://www.nngroup.com/articles/photos-as-web-content/>

10. Columbus, L, 2013,"IDC: 87% Of Connected Devices Sales By 2017 Will Be Tablets And Smartphones", <http://www.forbes.com/sites/louiscolumbus/2013/09/12/idc-87-of-connected-devices-by-2017-will-be-tablets-and-smartphones/>

11. AIMIA, 2015, "Australian mobile device ownership and home usage report"

12. Google, 2013, "What Users Want Most from Mobile Sites Today", <https://www.google.com.au/think/research-studies/what-users-want-most-from-mobile-sites-today.html>

13. Hubspot, 2013, "The ultimate list of marketing statistics", <http://www.hubspot.com/marketing-statistics>

14. Social Media News, 2015, "Social Media Statistics Australia", <http://www.socialmedianews.com.au/social-media-statistics-australia-may-2015/>

15. WPI Communications, 2013, "Dental Marketing Barometer Survey", <http://www.aaid.com/uploads/cms/documents/2013_dental_marketing_barometer_survey.pdf>

16. Social Media News, 2015, "Social Media Statistics Australia", <http://www.socialmedianews.com.au/social-media-statistics-australia-may-2015/>

17. YouTube, 2015, "YouTube statistics", <https://www.youtube.com/yt/press/en-GB/statistics.html>

18. Adelie Studios, 2015, "The Top 15 Video Marketing Statistics for 2015", <http://www.adeliestudios.com/top-15-video-marketing-statistics-2015/>

19. Mist Media & Maria, J, 2015, "45 Video Marketing Statistics" <http://www.virtuets.com/45-video-marketing-statistics/>

20. ComScore & Maria, J, 2015, "45 Video Marketing Statistics" <http://www.virtuets.com/45-video-marketing-statistics/>

21. MarketingProfs & Maria, J, 2015, "45 Video Marketing Statistics" <http://www.virtuets.com/45-video-marketing-statistics/>

22. ComScore & Maria, J, 2015, "45 Video Marketing Statistics" <http://www.virtuets.com/45-video-marketing-statistics/>

23. Wistia & Maria, J, 2015, "45 Video Marketing Statistics" <http://www.virtuets.com/45-video-marketing-statistics/>

24. Farris & Bendle, 2010, "Marketing Metrics: The Definitive Guide to Measuring Marketing Performance (2nd Edition)"

25. Murphy & Murphy, 2002, "Leading on the Edge of Chaos"

26. Lawrence, A, 2012, "Five Customer Retention Tips for Entrepreneurs", <http://www.forbes.com/sites/alexlawrence/2012/11/01/five-customer-retention-tips-for-entrepreneurs/>

27. Reichheld, F, 2000, "The Economics of E-Loyalty – HBS Working Knowledge" <http://hbswk.hbs.edu/archive/1590.html>

28. Palmer, P, 2012, "Where have our patients gone?", <https://primepractice.com.au/articles/where-have-our-patients-gone-the-top-10-reasons-why-patients-don-t-come-back-167>

29. Charlton, G, 2014, "Email remains the best digital channel for ROI", <https://econsultancy.com/blog/64614-email-remains-the-best-digital-channel-for-roi/>

30. Sound Results On Hold., 2015, "On hold statistics", <http://www.soundresultsonhold.com/on_hold_stats_studies.html>

31. Software of Excellence, 2014, "Achieving Optimum Recall Effectiveness in the Dental Practice"

32. Sensis, 2015, "Sensis Social Media Report May 2015", <https://www.sensis.com.au/assets/PDFdirectory/Sensis_Social_Media_Report_2015.pdf>

33. Schiff, A, 2013, "Dental office marketing budget review", <http://www.dentaleconomics.com/articles/print/volume-99/issue-4/features/dental-office-marketing-budget-review.html>

34. Wikipedia, 2015, "Rebate (marketing)", <https://en.wikipedia.org/wiki/Rebate_(marketing)>

35. People Pulse, 2015, "Survey Response Rates", <http://www.peoplepulse.com.au/Survey-Response-Rates.htm>

36. Ciotti, G, 2013, "10 Essential Tactics for Creating Valuable Customer Surveys", <http://www.helpscout.net/blog/customer-survey/>

37. Help Scout, 2015, "75 Customer Service Facts, Quotes & Statistics", <http://www.helpscout.net/75-customer-service-facts-quotes-statistics/>

38. Word of Mouth Marketing Australia, 2014, "Word of Mouth Marketing", <http://www.wommau.com/Word-of-mouth-marketing.htm>

39. Doyle, M, 2015, "The Top Three Digital Phenomena And Social Media Marketing Trends For 2015", <http://blog.twmg.com.au/category/online-trends/>

40. Gover, S, 2014, "Dealing with online negative reviews for your business", <http://www.iconvisual.com.au/about-us/news/dealing-with-online-negative-reviews-for-your-business>

41. Savage, R, 2010, "Patient-centric marketing", <http://www.dentaleconomics.com/articles/print/volume-100/issue-7/features/patient-centric-marketing.html>

42. SecurePay, 2014, "Online reviews: why you need them and how to manage them", <https://www.securepay.com.au/insights/articles/online-reviews-why-you-need-them-and-how-to-manage-them>

About The Author

About Carolyn S. Dean

Carolyn S. Dean is the author of *Fully Booked* and a widely known seminar speaker and dental marketing consultant who works extensively with dental professionals.

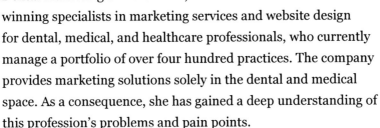

Carolyn is the Managing Director at My Dental Marketing and Wellsites, award-winning specialists in marketing services and website design for dental, medical, and healthcare professionals, who currently manage a portfolio of over four hundred practices. The company provides marketing solutions solely in the dental and medical space. As a consequence, she has gained a deep understanding of this profession's problems and pain points.

Carolyn has been involved in sales and marketing for over twenty-one years, working with some of the largest global IT organisations in the UK, USA, Europe, South Africa, Asia, and Australia. Over the last ten years, she has specialised in the dental, medical, and healthcare marketing.

In addition to her practical experience, Carolyn is the author of several business guides for health, medical, and dental practitioners and has contributed articles to a number of health, dental, and business publications. She has also spoken at various conferences and industry events on dental and medical marketing throughout Australia.

She lives with her husband and her two children in Sydney, Australia. When she is not looking after her family and businesses, she believes strongly in giving back to the community. She is a founding board member of The First Seeds Fund, who are committed to breaking the cycle of poverty and abuse that exists in areas of Australia.

Speaking engagements

Engage Carolyn to present a keynote or practical workshop at your next conference, meeting, team training, or event.

Carolyn can speak with authority on a range of dental marketing topics that appeal to both single practice owners and corporates, and for groups large and small.

Carolyn is renowned for being an inspiring presenter who shares practical skills and expertise so attendees can immediately implement what they've learnt to see real results.

Contact Carolyn to find out more

- On 02 9410 1507

- At http://fullybookeddentist.com/speaking

Find Out More

www.fullybookeddentist.com
www.mydentalmarketing.com.au

Facebook

www.facebook.com/CarolynSDean.Author
www.facebook.com/MyDentalMarketing

Twitter

@Carolyn_Dean
@MyDentalM

LinkedIn

www.linkedin.com/in/carolyndean

Instagram

@carolyn_s_dean

CPSIA information can be obtained
at www.ICGtesting.com
Printed in the USA
LVOW10s1336070218

565642LV00020B/170/P